LEARNING TO SEE

Go outside and look around,
See what you can see.
If you are unable to see anything beautiful,
anything that brings you peace,
a deep sense of joy and God's presence,
anything that delights you
with the magic of color and aliveness . . .
If you are not reminded that today is special,
a unique, once-in-a-lifetime gift from the Creator . . .
Then you need to spend more time outside,
and you need to read this book.

When I Relax I Feel Guilty

Tim Hansel

David C. Cook Publishing Co.

ELGIN, ILLINOIS—WESTON, ONTARIO

Scripture quotations, except where otherwise noted, are taken
from the J. B. Phillips translation (New Testament) and from
the Revised Standard Version (Old Testament).

Edited by Marshall Shelley
Cover design by Paul Thompson
Printed in the United States of America

ISBN 0-89191-137-5
LC 78-73460

First Printing, April 1979
93 92 91 90   25 24 23 22 21 20

CONTENTS

To mom and dad, two rascal saints,
who have touched so many lives, especially mine,
and who taught me to "work hard, pray hard, and play hard";
To Pam, who has given my life meaning I never knew existed;
To Zachary and Joshua, my midget gurus of play;
To the Lord of Creation, who created everything,
even rest.

SLOW ME DOWN, LORD

Slow me down, Lord.

Ease the pounding of my heart by the
quieting of my mind.

Steady my hurried pace with a vision of
the eternal reach of time.

Give me, amid the confusion of the day,
the calmness of the everlasting hills.

Break the tensions of my nerves and
muscles with the soothing music of the
singing streams that live in my memory.

Teach me the art of taking minute
vacations—of slowing down to look at a
flower, to chat with a friend, to pat a dog,
to smile at a child, to read a few lines
from a good book.

Slow me down, Lord, and inspire me to
send my roots deep into the soil of life's enduring
values, that I may grow toward my greater destiny.

Remind me each day that the race is not
always to the swift; that there is more to life
than increasing its speed.

Let me look upward to the towering oak
and know that it grew great and strong
because it grew slowly and well.

Rev. Wilferd A. Peterson

Hope is enough   Hope is not enough

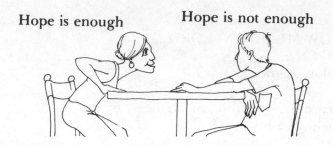

Love is enough   Love is not enough

Faith is enough   Faith is not enough

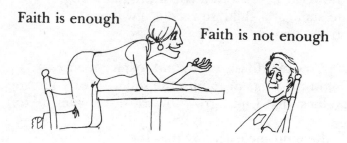

Enough is enough!   Enough is not enough.

—Courtesy of Jim Carlson

PREFACE

HOLD IT! IS YOUR LIFE going too fast these days? Is it evidenced by the fact that you just raced past the poem a couple pages back, entitled, ironically enough, "Slow Me Down, Lord"?

Just looking at it isn't enough. The words you glance at don't count—only the ones you digest. It's much like eating. The problem in our society is not that we don't eat (or read, or do) enough, but that we eat too much, too often, too quickly—and use too little.

Is it possible that your days are hurrying by so fast that you don't fully taste them anymore? Are *play* and *rest* foreign words in your living vocabulary? When was the last time you flew a kite, went for a bike ride, or made

11

something with your hands? When was the last time you caught yourself enjoying life so deeply that you couldn't quite get the smile off your face?

Chances are, it's been too long.

I never cease to be amazed at the incredible paradox of seeing so many unhappy people in a world that has so much to offer. What surprises me even more is the sight of so many Christians who have succumbed to busyness, unhappiness, tightness, and boredom. Many suffer from a nagging sense of guilt that no matter how much they do, it is never quite enough.

Leisure has become a word with bad connotations, implying comfort, convenience, and complacency. Many try to resolve their guilt and frustration by working harder and longer, but the feeling of imprisonment remains. The result is both subtle and devastating.

In our worthy attempt to avoid idleness and questionable pleasures, we begin to feel that everything must be useful. Thus, our false guilt compels us to read for profit, attend parties for contacts, exercise so we can work better, and rest in order to be more efficient. We regress to a kind of neopuritanism that says, "You have not been born into the world for pleasure." A curious and familiar psychological need to justify everything emerges, leaving no room for discovery and pure enjoyment.

Words like *wonder, joy, rest,* and *freedom* have become faded replicas of what Christ taught. Time becomes a tyrant instead of a friend. Joy becomes something we will do later. Play becomes something for children. Creativity becomes the unattainable quality of artists and poets instead of the essence of our lives. Wonder is just the name of a bread, and imagination doesn't make enough money to be worthwhile.

Most people conform, becoming safe, careful, sensible nonindividuals who are incapable of taking chances.

Sadly, without risk, there is no real joy. Our watered-down gospel of prudence, caution, and familiar (if busy) routine becomes suffocating dullness. Then we resort to all kinds of things to make us happy—which never quite succeed. The simple joy of existence seems ever more distant and evasive.

No book can promise to be the key to happiness, but it can breathe some fresh air into your life. It can uproot some of the habits and social pressures that inhibit the full expression of commitment to Christ—commitment with abandon. It can shed light on the essential purpose of being alive—to know God, glorify, and enjoy him forever.

What does this mean in daily life? What is important? Are there some alternatives we don't usually think of?

The first thing we need to recognize is that we live in an amphibian world of both work and leisure. To look at one without the other is blindness. They are complementary. Although the primary thrust of this book is to emancipate us from our pallid concepts of leisure, it will necessarily have to challenge some of our superficial views of work.

In the end, the result will be not only a deeper understanding of both but also a reconciliation of the two in our own life-styles. As we uncover the deeper purposes of both, hopefully God will invade our lives at a level more profound than we've ever experienced before.

This book has already changed at least one life—my own. While working on the manuscript, I felt as if God were reintroducing himself to me in dimensions I never knew existed before. This has been a significant time for me, a season of unusual and previously untasted joy. My prayer is that something here will touch you, and that you will recognize again and again that the whole of your life, without any exception, can become an act of worship.

This book is divided into three sections. Part 1, "Enough Is Not Enough," deals with our dislocated images of work and leisure. Part 2, "Enough Is Enough," presents a renewed harmony between work and leisure and the uniqueness of the Christian position. Part 3, "Enough Is More than Enough," will emphasize the practical, showing specific ways to creative, quality leisure. But essentially, this book has a single aim:

To give you permission
to give yourself permission
to enjoy yourself more,
to enjoy others more,
and to enjoy God more than you ever imagined.

Many friends deserve thanks for the help and support that allowed this book to be written. In particular, I wish to express my appreciation to these people:

To Sandra Phelps, who visited me when I was in the hospital in San Diego. Her ideas and encouragement at that time were instrumental in the completion of this book.

To Irma Brito, whose stamina on a typewriter goes unmatched.

To Ron Wilson and Marshall Shelley, whose unyielding patience and enthusiasm were always coupled with creative ideas on how to make this dream come true. Their skill as editors and writers and their contagious commitment to Christ are hidden on many pages of this book.

To the staff of Summit Expedition—Dennis White, Jeff Cooper, Jill Stanley, Beth Block, Fred Hurst, and Bob Blumenthal—who so willingly put in extra hours so I could stay at the typewriter.

To Jim Baker, whose insights while reading the manuscript were not only encouraging but also helpful in shaping the final outcome.

Finally, to my family, who came out to my study often enough to remind me that I was a husband and father first of all, and who, through it all, taught me the reasons for joy that are found on these pages.

Part 1
Enough Is Not Enough

Unbearable mental fatigue. Work alone could rest me; gratuitous work, or play . . . I am far from that. Each thought becomes an anxiety in my brain. I am becoming the ugliest of all things: a busy man.

Andre Gide

1
WEARY SERVANTS
OF THE
IMPOSSIBLE

The Christian life is not difficult . . . it is impossible.
I can't live it; I'm never surprised when I fail.

Howard Butt
The Velvet Covered Brick

If I had only . . . forgotten future greatness
and looked at the green things and the buildings
and reached out to those around me
and smelled the air
and ignored the forms and the self-styled obligations
and heard the rain on my roof
and put my arms around my wife
. . . perhaps it's not too late.

Hugh Prather
Notes to Myself

LEISURE HAS ALWAYS BEEN DIFFICULT for me to incorporate into my life. I have rarely been accused of working too little. My problem has been just the opposite. Overwork is one of the greatest problems for sincere, dedicated Christians today, and I have often been guilty

19

of it. How, then, am I qualified to write a book on leisure? The answer is, I am not. Yet that, strangely enough, may prove beneficial because, as you will soon see, I know by experience (a lot of it) the consequences of overwork and busyness.

Play came quite naturally when I was young. In fact, I was accused of overwhelming others with my enthusiasm for play. But something happened. I can remember "growing old" in my early twenties. Work had always been highly esteemed in our family, and hard work was seen as the primary tool for success. I figured if it were good to work ten hours, it would be even better to work fourteen.

In college, I seemed to have the energy to withstand the pressure. I remember times at Stanford when I wouldn't even go home at night. Instead, I would push a table up near the door of the cafeteria at 3 A.M. and sleep on it, using my books as a pillow. And then in the morning, when I had to be at work, the first person to open the door would knock me off the table, and I'd wake up and start the day. I convinced myself that I was sleeping "faster" than anyone else.

I had summer jobs that started at five in the morning and lasted until eight at night. I can remember mom getting up a little after 4 A.M. to fix enormous quantities of eggs and bacon and toast and milk to supply the energy for me to make it through the day. These were special times, important times, and without a doubt, valuable times. But over the years, they did something to my priorities. Work gradually filtered to the top.

During the years when I was a coach and an area director for Young Life, I would work twelve, fourteen, even fifteen hours a day, six or seven days a week. And I would come home feeling that I hadn't worked enough. So I tried to cram even more into my schedule. I spent more time promoting living than I did living. I never knew what Christ meant when he said, "Come to me, all of you who are weary and overburdened, and I will give you rest! Put on my yoke and learn from me. For I am gentle and humble in heart and you will find rest for your souls. For my yoke is easy and my burden is light" (Matt. 11:28-30). My life wasn't abundant; it was a frantic sprint from one hour to the next.

I can remember times when fatigue left me feeling isolated and alienated—feelings that previously had been foreigners to me. Unprepared for such parasites on my energy, I became frustrated, and laughter, which had always been my most treasured companion, had silently slipped away. In 1973, I wrote in my journal:

When laughter fades
    the tendency is toward self-absorption
        and the iris of life's eye
squeezes the light to a pinpoint.

Morning only intimidates you into another day
    and creativity no longer has the energy to care.

In the midst of this season of my life, I received a letter from a girl I'd been dating whom I loved very much (and who a few years later became my wife and mother of my children). In this letter, she included the quotation from the journals of Andre Gide that appeared at the beginning of Part 1.

It was a perfect description of what I'd become—the ugliest of all things: a busy man. The words were so painfully true that I *worked* hard to undo their grip on me. And for a short time, I succeeded. The burden of guilt about not working enough was lifted. But deeply ingrained habits don't just disappear. Eventually they

21

surface in other forms. Before long, I was rushing ahead as frenetically as ever.

I was dominated by "shoulds," "ought to's," and "musts." I would awaken unrefreshed in the morning, with a tired kind of resentment, and hurry through the day trying to uncover and meet the demands of others. Days were not lived but endured. I was exhausted trying to be a hope constantly rekindled for others, straining to live up to their images of me. I had worked hard to develop a reputation as one who was concerned, available, and involved—now I was being tyrannized by it. Often I was more at peace in the eyes of others than in my own.

The Western mind and culture leave little time for leisure, prayer, play, and contemplation. Hurry needs answers; answers need categories; categories need labeling and dissecting. The pace I was trying to maintain had no time for rhythm and awe, for mystery and wonder. I barely had time to care adequately for friends or for myself. In order to keep up my incessant activity, God was simply reduced to fit into my schedule. I suffered, because he didn't fit.

Many of our sins are caused by hurry and thoughtlessness. No matter how "good" our purpose is, a driven man is still enslaved. He cannot act freely, thoughtfully, lovingly. The good becomes the enemy of the best. Henry David Thoreau offered first prize to the man who can live one day deliberately. But this is not an easily accomplished task. Quiet minds, which are established in stillness, refuse to be perplexed or intimidated. They are like a clock in a thunderstorm, which moves at its own pace.

Slowly the flywheel was turning, and I was discovering that if I wanted to be truly, radically committed to Jesus Christ, I would have to stop doing at least some of what I

was doing in order to do the other part well, with a
liveliness of faith and the contagion of love.

Journal entries at this time indicated my readiness:

> I want my life . . . to be more than just work.

> The task now
> is to live
> what I was going to say.

> I am weary to the bone of talking "about life," of
> showing pictures "about life," of reading "about
> life." It's time for a change.

> Few men have cared enough to defy these hurried
>   values; fewer still have the detachment, the
>   courage and commitment to establish themselves
>   in the timeless priorities that I am finding in the
>   Scriptures,
>   to risk the consequences of a life-style that is
>   deliberately chosen rather than just
>   accepted.

It appeared I was at a spiritual intersection. I had to
choose between apparent "success," which meant living
up to someone else's standards, or true contentment in
my own uniqueness, based on a deep and radical kind of
self-acceptance imbedded in the unconditional love of
Christ. I chose to believe, in more than just words, that
what I am is more important than what I do.

Hurry gives us an "excuse" for our lack of spiritual
growth. Only by breaking the chains of busyness can we
escape the prison of status quo, and experience a life that
draws ever nearer to God.

In seeking a pattern for such a life-style, I had to look

in the direction of a simple carpenter who gave Energy
not its name but its power. When he said, "Be perfect,
even as your Father in heaven is perfect" (Mt. 5:48,
TLB), he wasn't talking about the perfectionism that I
had been trying to achieve, but rather a quality of wholeness that I had never tasted before. He was asking me to
be indelible rather than impeccable. He called for a
depth of maturity that bases its actions in personal self-
worth more than how many records one holds. It does
not come as a bludgeon to condemn us, but as an affirma-
tion to set us free. The key question was "In what do I
place my confidence?"

I didn't want to end up like one of my journal entries:

> She was very pretty,
> very clever,
>   and very adept in the social arena
> and had about as much depth of character as a pie
> tin.

I realized again that we don't take God's name in vain
as much with our lips as with our lives. I sought to know
the reality and substance of the living Christ at levels I
had never known before.

In my reading I was drawn to authors who would help
light the way. M. C. Richards, in her graceful book called
Centering, expressed it well: "I enjoy myself most when I
am so at peace that activity is secondary. . . . I also know
how difficult it is to develop this as habit; necessitating a
strong and graceful, persistent discipline of priorities—
and a heart which consistently yields itself to its Source.
Centering is the image I use for the process of balance
which enables us to step along that thread feeling it not as
a thread but as a sphere. It will, it is hoped, help us to walk
through the necessary extremes with an incorruptible

instinct for wholeness. . . . This thread can be as limber as breath. It can be as tough as a wild grape vine."[1]

As I began to unfetter myself from some of the excessive hurry and overwork, I discovered that I wasn't really giving up anything. In turn, I was able to enjoy my days and achievements as never before. By 1976, my journal entries had a different personality:

> Today
>   one which I've never lived before
>   and one which I will never get to live again.
> Thank you, Lord, for this incredible gift. The surprise of unwrapping it holds wonder and the privilege of excitement.
>
> By creation . . . I am.
> And that is enough.

The journey has been my teacher in so many ways, and our Lord has been faithful in persistently translating my incessant doing into a deeper sense of being. The process is still far from over in my life—I still struggle with life's hectic velocity. In fact no one (except a lean and lonely carpenter some years back) has ever come close to living at a godly pace. All of us will fail at times—we are servants of the impossible. But our goal is in the journey, in coming closer.

And as I look back over my footprints, I am grateful for the stamina of God.

2
COMMITTED
TO JOY

What then is the chief end of man?
Man's chief end is to glorify God and to enjoy him forever.
        The Westminster Larger Catechism, 1861

ENDANGERED SPECIES HAS BECOME an oft-used term in recent years, usually referring to threatened animals. Yet one of the rarest species on the face of the earth may soon become extinct without anyone even recognizing its passing—namely, those few human beings who truly know how to enjoy life.

They glorify God not only with their words but even more with their lives. They enjoy God for who he is, not just for what he can do for them. To them, each day holds its own reward. They know that each twenty-four hours is a once-in-a-lifetime privilege and that happiness is a by-product of quality living. Their lives are lived according to their priorities, in spite of the consequences. They live life from the inside out.

This endangered species has been called "the earthy mystics" or the "disciplined wild man." Nikos Kazantakis calls him Zorba—"Like the child, he sees everything for the first time. He is forever astonished and wonders why and wherefore. Everything seems miraculous . . . each morning when he opens his eyes he sees trees, sea, stones and birds, and is amazed."[1] He has cracked through the thin crust we call civilization to find the supernatural substance upon which life rests.

If we had more people like that, we wouldn't need a book such as this. Yet our bookstores are glutted with books on how to be happy. The pursuit of happiness has become our nation's number one industry. We spend more on leisure and recreation each year than we do on education, construction of new homes, or national defense. The latest figures compiled by *U.S. News and World Report* show that Americans will spend more than $160 billion on leisure and recreation this year. By 1985, the total is expected to be $300 billion. But will doubling our spending double our pleasure? Probably not.

The pursuit of pleasure has always been a most unhappy quest. Despite more money and time being spent on leisure, the suicide rate among young people (the second leading cause of death among that age) has gone up 25 percent, and our mental hospital population is on a steady rise.

What's going wrong? How is it that we can spend so much time and money and energy and still be profoundly unhappy?

PRACTICING BEING UNHAPPY

Part of the problem may be clarified by a statement I overheard a few months ago while leaving an airplane. A large man from Texas was nudging his way down the aisle talking to the woman in front of him. As they passed me, he was saying, "Well, that's the real problem, you see.

ENOUGH IS NOT ENOUGH

Most people spend their whole lives practicing being unhappy."

He's right. Many people seem determined to be unimpressed with life. Somehow it's not proper to enjoy life, to feel excitement, to be content. Advertisers subtly infect us with their message that we cannot be happy until we buy their product. And when we do, it doesn't change our lives, but then, we hardly notice because we're being told about another new product we simply *must* have. Thus we continue our art of practicing unhappiness.

Walter Kerr begins his book, *The Decline of Pleasure,* by saying, "I'm going to start out by assuming that you are approximately as unhappy as I am. Neither of us may be submitting ourselves to psychiatrists, neither of us may take an excessive number of tranquilizers each day, neither of us may have married three times in an effort to find someone to make us happier. We are not (quite yet) desperate, but we are, vaguely, dissatisfied. . . . We are vaguely wretched because we are living half lives, half-heartedly, and with only one half of our minds actively engaged in making contact with the universe around us."[2]

What can we do about this half-alive infection? That is what this book is about. To overcome the problem, we need to understand how to live life fully, to accept the time we have been given, and to enjoy it. We will need to understand both work and leisure.

THE PROBLEM OF LEISURE

Most people in our society go into each week with more nonworking hours than working hours. We have longer weekends, shorter workweeks, and paid vacations from two to three, even to four weeks. Some people have even more. But most of us do not know how to handle leisure.

Why don't we give it more meaning, since it is in fact most of our life? There are a number of things to consider. One is our deeply ingrained, sometimes blind devotion to work. Another is our inability to understand the true meaning and purpose of leisure.

To many, the word *leisure* has an unsubstantial sound. It is like smoke through our fingers. It confuses us, and therefore we mistrust it. Picture postcards cast magic glamour over places to go and things to do, but the nature and essence of true leisure still eludes us. Often this confusion makes us turn leisure into work. Motivated by a false sense of guilt, we transform what should be a joyous weekend release into a Monday-morning exhaustion. We turn pleasurable games into hard-fought contests.

We have yet to learn that true leisure is not idleness, and that leisure is each man's touchstone with himself and his inner resources. We haven't yet decided how much value to give to the leisure in our lives. As a result, we don't know how to put it in a proper balance with work.

> **leisure** (lezh-ur) *noun* freedom, rest opportunity, time, unhurried quietude, peace, relaxation, stillness, repose, peace, composure of manner, quiet ease and dignity of bearing, calm, reprieve, interval.

Part of the confusion about leisure is the result of using as synonyms a number of overlapping and ill-defined terms such as *play, game,* and *recreation.* Another difficulty lies in the fact that some define leisure as a certain type of *activity,* while others define it as a *state of mind.* One tradition conceives of leisure as free time not devoted to paid occupations. The other, much older, classical tradition conceives of leisure as cultivation of the self and a preoccupation with the higher values of life.

If you will excuse me a moment for not speaking English, I think you will find it helpful to know the background of the word *leisure.* It comes from the Latin word *licere,* which means "to be permitted." More today than ever, we need to learn how to give ourselves permission to relax, to play, to enjoy life, and to enjoy God for who he is.

It's interesting that the Latin word for work was *negotium,* or "nonleisure." Work was thus secondary, defined as it related to leisure. Our society does just the opposite, defining leisure as "nonwork." We tend to be almost compulsively utilitarian. Everything must contribute to our work. We play in order to work better or to be more "useful" to God. In many ways, these are the habits that keep us unhappy. In our myopia of overvalued productivity, we have forgotten how to enjoy things for what they are.

The Greeks also stressed the centrality of leisure, but they added another important facet. The Greek word for work was *ascholia,* which means absence of leisure. The word for leisure was *schole,* which leads to the English words *school* and *scholarship.* Leisure, then, was a time for growth and development.

Someone once defined leisure as "an attitude of mind and a condition of the soul that fosters a capacity to perceive the reality of the world." Jesus Christ said, "I am the light of the world. The man who follows me will never walk in the dark but will live his life in the light" (John 8:12). Leisure can, if we permit it, become an intersection of the timeless qualities of life. Prayer, *recreatio mentis in*

Deum ("the recreation of the soul in God"), is necessarily an act of leisure. Play, when our spirits finally respond to Jesus' command to be more childlike, is an expression of not only the value of leisure, but of life itself. And love, if it ever becomes "work," will become imprisoned and powerless, and the greatest shaping force on earth will be lost.

Leisure is more than just nonwork. It is a point of contact with reality and a catalyst for new experiences, new ideas, new people, and new places. It is the time when the gift of wholeness again becomes a hope and a possibility.

In order for this to happen, three things must be done. First, we must be convinced of the importance of quality leisure in our lives—not superficial play, but true *licere* and *schole*. Second, we must understand how to practice quality leisure. We cannot assume it will just happen. It doesn't. Third, we must then act on what we know to be true. This is both the difficult part and the most exciting. Reading a book on the subject is not enough. We cannot afford to be hearers only. It must be lived. "Don't stare at my fingers—look where I'm pointing."

This takes effort, courage, and discipline, as well as a little craziness. As Zorba said, "Boss, you've got everything except one thing—Madness! A man needs a little madness or else he never dares cut the rope to be free."[3]

3

THE WORTH
OF WORK

*This book, being about work, is, by its very nature, about
violence—to the spirit as well as to the body. It is about ulcers as
well as accidents. About shouting matches as well as fist fights.
About nervous breakdowns as well as kicking the dog around. It
is, above all (or beneath all), about daily humiliations. To
survive the day is triumph enough.*

Studs Terkel
Working

EXCEPT FOR HEADLINE GRABBERS such as union demands and teacher strikes, we generally do not think of
work as a controversial subject. But it is.

Work has been receiving more and more attention
these days. Ironically, though this century has produced
unusual opportunities for leisure, it is also known (and
condemned) for being the fastest. In a strange twist,
technology relieves us of work but adds to our busyness.
We have been relieved of labor without being relieved of
the historic assumption that only labor is meaningful. We

feel guilty for working so hard, because we've been told that meaningful lives depend upon pausing for pleasure. These incompatible guilts produce tremendous pressure.

What is the purpose of work? What is its proper emphasis? Consider the tension between the following interpretations of work. Where do you stand? Or are you one of those who has never "had the time" to think it through? For God's sake (literally) and for yours, slow down a minute to see how your views compare to the following views of work.

* * *

"Most middle-class Americans tend to worship their work, to work at their play, and to play at their worship. As a result, their meanings and values are distorted. Their relationships disintegrate faster than they can keep them in repair, and their life-styles resemble a cast of characters in search of a plot" (Gordon Dahl).[1]

* * *

"There is a perennial nobleness, and even sacredness in work. . . . In idleness alone is there perpetual despair. . . . A man perfects himself by working. All work, even cotton spinning, is noble. Work alone is noble" (Thomas Carlyle).[2]

* * *

"They talk of the dignity of work, bosh. The dignity is in the leisure" (Herman Melville).[3]

* * *

ENOUGH IS NOT ENOUGH

"We don't consider manual work as a curse, or a bitter necessity, not even as a means of making a living. We consider it as a high human function. As a basis of human life. The most dignified thing in the life of a human being and which ought to be free, creative. Men ought to be proud of it" (David Ben-Gurion).[4]

* * *

"The laboring man has not leisure for a true integrity day by day. He has no time but to be anything but a machine" (Henry David Thoreau).[5]

* * *

"Possibly the greatest malaise in our country today is our neurotic compulsion to work" (William McNamara).[6]

* * *

Where is the truth? I'm the first to admit the difficulties in sorting out a proper perspective of work, and that no one can deal with the subject comprehensively. However, we do need to identify and break through some of the common myths about work that are so prevalent in our culture. This is a delicate issue, because it challenges us at a basic level of our life-styles. Because we are imbued with the strong work ethic, our identity has in many cases been limited to what we do between the hours of eight and five.

Think about that for a moment. How are men ranked and rewarded in a democratic society? It is usually on the basis of their accomplishments at work. If a stranger approaches and asks, "Who are you?" how do you reply? The odds are that after offering your name and where you are from, you will identify yourself in terms of your work. So will nearly everyone else. In our culture, work has become one of the biggest factors in determining personal identity. It is not surprising, therefore, that work is often assigned universal and unqualified value. It becomes a basis for measuring human worth.

The problem is that work, in and of itself, does not have the intrinsic value to deserve such veneration. This is coupled with the fact that less than half of our society works. And, as a result of the combination of shorter workweeks and longer vacations, the average American worker today has nearly twelve hundred more hours of nonworking time per year than did his grandfather living before the turn of the century.

Therefore, what we need particularly at this point in our history is a new philosophy of work because for many people, work alone will be inadequate for the full expression of their identity, their freedom, and their human dignity. We will also need more regular occasions for play and creative leisure in order to experience the mystery and wonder of being alive.

Yes, work is both good and necessary. It should be pursued with diligence, honesty, and pride. But it should not be worshiped and glorified as the basis of human dignity and worth. People are valuable totally apart from their job productivity. Work never saved anyone from sin, death, or evil, nor has it ever unilaterally produced faith, hope, and love. When work becomes a person's all-consuming interest, even if the work is good and necessary, it is idolatry.

For most of us, however, work is an inescapable fact of life—it is the way we obtain the physical necessities of existence. As someone said, "God asks no man whether or not he will accept life. The choice is how." The same seems to hold true for work. The central question is not whether or not to work, but our attitude towards our work. Shall we allow it to be the center of our lives? Shall we continue to allow our individual identity to be determined by a career?

These are not just philosophical questions. They take on flesh and blood under both blue collars and white collars. "I'm a machine," says the factory worker. "I'm just unpaid labor," says the housewife. "I'm an object," says the fashion model. "I'm caged," says the bank teller.

How should we approach work? Scripture, for example, affirms work as a gift from God (Eccles. 3:13), but two chapters later warns that unless we have the power to enjoy it, it is all vanity and striving after wind. The Bible suggests that work is good, but when compared to eternal things, it can be hollow. In fact, sometimes it points out that work gets in the way of salvation.

Jesus would not have been a good promoter for the work ethic. Not only did he leave his own job as a carpenter, but he also called other people away from their jobs. He preached about the dangers of becoming preoccupied with work and the pursuit of wealth and power. He told a rich young man to sell all his possessions and give the proceeds to the poor—hardly a wise investment of capital from a businessman's viewpoint.

Likewise the early church remembered what Jesus had said about the birds of the air—"They never sow nor reap nor store away in barns, and yet your Heavenly Father feeds them. Aren't you much more valuable to him than they are?" (Matt. 6:26). Early Christians put much greater emphasis on personal salvation than they did analyzing trends, making long-range projections, and worrying about budgets. Their first priority was to grow closer to God. Work, in a sense, was something they did in their free time.

I should say again that this is not a treatise against

work, but against overwork. It is an attempt to counteract the sometimes blind loyalty to work that frequently causes us to have false and superficial ideas about ourselves, our families, our leisure, and our Creator. Therefore, let's identify nine of the common notions about work that we need to be aware of. Pointing out the myths is the first step in overcoming them.

- Work is the primary source of your identity.
- Work is inherently good, and therefore, the more work you do, the better person you are.
- You are not really serving the Lord unless you consistently push to the point of fatigue.
- The more you work, the more God loves you.
- If you work hard enough fifty weeks a year, then you "deserve" a two-week vacation.
- The purpose of work is to make enough money to buy things so you can be happy.
- Most of your problems would be solved if you would only work harder.
- The Bible says that the most important thing a person can do is to work.
- The biggest problem in our society is that people don't work hard enough.

Unless we are willing to take a hard look at some of the myths we cherish, we will continue to be, sometimes unknowingly, their slave. Clear vision is impossible unless we are willing to clean out the underbrush of assumptions that we have allowed to grow wild.

Many of us may feel a vague frustration because we sense our lives starting to atrophy—and we can't identify the cause. In many cases, it is due to a preoccupation with work that blurs the things that are truly important—my relationship to God, my health, my family, my personal growth, and my friends.

The central question remains: what is the meaning and

purpose of life? If we, as Christians, do not demonstrate as well as speak a different reply than the world around us, then where is our message? If we try to rationalize our compulsive work habits by saying we are accomplishing things for God, then, logically, we aren't *anything* unless we are *doing* something. To make matters worse, we have taken these workaholic habits beyond the realm of work to include our personal, social, and spiritual lives as well. In our attempts to make our deeper commitments more "useful," we slowly become mere functionaries. Our prayer life becomes only a time to ask God to do things for us, so that we can be better workers for him. The purpose and privilege of simply "knowing him and enjoying him forever" is considered unproductive. Our marriages slide quietly into what we can do for each other—the husband becoming a lawn mower and garbage remover, and the wife only keeping the house clean and the kids quiet. Children's usefulness is unclear, and in a culture infatuated with practicality, kids begin to see themselves as worthless. Friends are recognized as opportunities, and therefore a justifiable expenditure of time. And religion becomes a pattern of rules and regulations, a system that helps us tidy up our behavior, somewhat like rearranging the deck chairs on the Titanic. It allows us a better view as we go down.

Hence, the ramifications of our work ethic, and thus also our leisure ethic, are both more subtle and more devastating than one would first guess. We cannot afford the luxury of letting someone else decide how we should think on these issues. The inevitable consequence will be the erosion of joy.

When I first approached the subject of this book, I confess that my first concern was that it was not about a topic vital enough. The subject hasn't changed, but I surely have. The more I have studied it and tried to live it, the more I realized how closely it is tied to the essence of Christian living. A quality life demands quality work and quality leisure. But above all, it demands us giving ourselves permission to live fuller, deeper, more daring lives.

4
MYTHS
OF LEISURE

Faith has lost its joy. . . . Where everything must be useful and used, faith tends to regard its own freedom as good for nothing. It tries to make itself "useful" and in doing so often gambles away its freedom. Where freedom of play has been lost, the world turns into a desert.

Jurgen Moltmann
The Theology of Play

And the wind shall say:
Here were a decent godless people;
Their only monument
an asphalt road
and a thousand lost golf balls.

T. S. Eliot

WHAT ARE THE FIRST THINGS you think of when someone says the word *leisure*? What kind of images does it bring to mind?

We live in a world so crowded with images that we have to sort through them daily. Largely because of our media, leisure has come to connote comfort, convenience, luxury, something planned by someone else, styled in accordance with someone else's view of what produces happiness, usually dependent upon material things, void of creativity and involvement, opposed to risk, and rather insulated from the environment. It is, above all else, fun, easy, and expensive. It will meet our needs even though we aren't sure what they are, and it only requires approximately two weeks out of the year. This assumes two of the most basic messages of our media—you must go somewhere in order to be happy, and you must buy something.

This poses a lot of problems. The first is so many people believe they can't afford leisure, so they put it off into the future and live that life of suspended anticipation, habitually making plans for a special event that is always in the future. Life is always a rehearsal and they never quite get on stage. They can never quite afford it. Enough is never quite enough. And since we have, and sometimes even cherish, such false prefabricated ideas of what leisure really is, it remains an illusion. Since we hold such high and expensive and materialistic expectations of what leisure should be, life never seems to be able to match it.

This brings us to a second myth, which is, in some ways, even more pathetic. In this situation we watch all the commercials, read all the articles, dream all the dreams, and then even go so far as to save all the money. We work extra jobs to make sure that we'll have enough money to really have fun this time. And then by the time our vacation arrives, we are in such a hurry to have fun that we actually suffocate the hours with our expectations. Unable to relax, we can't really enjoy the gift of time we've been given, and all too soon we discover ourselves back at work. Predefined happiness never seems to quite come alive. The result is that we end up with an imitation vacation that looks like a vacation and sounds like a vacation and sometimes even feels like one, but it just doesn't taste right. Pasted-on happiness usually washes off in the first rain.

Young people, in particular, who have seen all too much of such empty pursuits, tend to equate the word *leisure* with hollowness, apathy, and lack of joy. They become uninterested in any kind of leisure pursuit because one of the greatest problems with leisure is that it is called leisure. It conjures up images of pudgy bodies being catered to and insulated from any direct exposure to environment and emotion.

BIONIC CHRISTIANS

There is another myth, peculiarly common among some Christians, that we don't deserve leisure. Some view leisure as a right rather than a gift, but others view it as superfluous and wasteful. It's the elder-brother syndrome—the compulsively responsible, upright, uptight citizen who continually tries to repeat the atonement instead of accepting it. This posture is one of restraint, denial, seriousness, almost martialed control, frugality of everything, including emotions.

At the school where I teach, this myth is humorously referred to as Bionic Christianity. It describes the super Christian who is, at least in appearance, above reproach. He has been redeemed, even of his humanness, and he works hard daily to earn his righteousness. Each of his answers is quick and precise, and his time is managed with calculated economy. Above all else, no time should be wasted on such frivolous things as laughter and play when there is so much to be done in the world. Heavily laden with guilt and tension about each of the minutes he might be wasting—stiff, fussy, meticulous, and incurably religious—the Bionic Christian simply does not have time to be happy. Irony of ironies, his commitment to Jesus Christ has become a prison rather than a blessing. So blinded by religious observations and reservations, he fails to see the festivity that was so central in the life of Jesus. He forgets that Jesus, despite the sad world he inhabited, was the prime host and the prime guest of the party. Jesus let himself be doused with perfume. He attended to wedding wine and wedding garments.

The Bible is full of merriment. The feast outruns the fast. It is crammed with spitted kids and lambs and fatted calves, grapes, pomegranates, olives, dates, milk, and honey.[1]

Can believers learn how to relax, play, and even celebrate in the midst of today's obvious chaos? How can a committed person enjoy leisure amid the tapestry of pain we view on the evening news each night? Many Christians agonize over this question, perhaps even more than in preceding ages because of the constant media exposure—the early disciples didn't know about famine in India or earthquakes in Guatemala. The impact of world tensions and problems is often so great that many believers, because they feel and care more than non-believers, frequently tend to become overanxious and exaggerate their own responsibilities. We all need to be reminded that God is by no means bewildered by today's situation any more than he was at the time of Christ.

We also need to be encouraged frequently to look at the whole of Scripture. Too often we get myopic and selective in our reading, seeking information only to affirm our preconceived notions. Fortunately, Scripture will not allow us to neutralize its overwhelming message of grace. For although it is a library of nations and indi-

ENOUGH IS NOT ENOUGH

viduals torn and divided; although its pages ache with chastening affliction and despair; these are consistently overpowered by a God of grace. Scripture does not hide the hollow places of doubt and emptiness; it includes the jealousy of fasters who condemn the feasters. Yet the Bible is still very clear in its celebration of life.

Because many of us still feel guilty, we apply the work ethic to our leisure experiences lest we be thought of as lazy. We vacillate between self-assertion and self-depreciation, always trying to earn the gift of joy. When will we learn that the meaning of Easter lies in the liberation from such images?

BREAKING THE SPELL

How do we break the spell and accept the invitation to a freer life-style? The first step is by letting go of the attitudes that would have us continually deny our health and happiness in an effort to be responsible. Let go of the fears of inconvenience. Let go of the need to constantly compare. Let go of some of the warm, comfortable, colorless, tasteless, abstract images you have of leisure, and leap out of some of your routines. Begin to refresh yourself in some of the simple joys of being alive. Turn off your TV for a while and experience again the thrill of living your life directly rather than vicariously, without all the baggage and parachutes. Some of us need to read the following letter written by an anonymous friar in a monastery in Nebraska late in his life. We probably not only need to read it, but we need to allow it to seep down into the marrow of our tired and serious bones.

If I had my life to live over again, I'd try

to make more mistakes next time.
I would relax, I would limber up, I would be sillier
than I have been this trip.
I know of very few things I would take seriously.
I would take more trips. I would be crazier.
I would climb more mountains, swim more rivers,
and watch more sunsets.
I would do more walking and looking.
I would eat more ice cream and less beans.
I would have more actual troubles, and fewer
imaginary ones.
You see, I'm one of those people who lives life
prophylactically and sensibly hour after hour,
day after day. Oh, I've had my moments, and if I
had to do it over again I'd have more of them.
In fact, I'd try to have nothing else, just moments,
one after another, instead of living so many years
ahead each day. I've been one of those people
who never go anywhere without a thermometer, a
hot-water bottle, a gargle, a raincoat, aspirin, and
a parachute.
If I had to do it over again I would go places, do
things, and travel lighter than I have.
If I had my life to live over I would start barefooted
earlier in the spring and stay that way later in the
fall.
I would play hookey more.
I wouldn't make such good grades, except by
accident.
I would ride on more merry-go-rounds.
I'd pick more daisies.

Let go. Take a chance. As Ben Franklin said, "There's a
time to wink as well as to see." Breaking the spell requires
risk and abandonment. But who ever said it was safe to

follow Jesus Christ? He has a most annoying manner of showing up when we least want him; of confronting us in the strangest ways; of popping the balloons that we were hiding behind in order to prove again to us that this abundant life he spoke about is more than just a good idea. He is the messenger of not only good news but unexpected news as well.

Part 2
Enough Is Enough

A real Christian is an odd number, anyway. He feels supreme love for One whom he has never seen; talks familiarly every day to Someone he cannot see; expects to go to heaven on the virtue of Another; empties himself in order to be full; admits he is wrong so he can be declared right; goes down in order to get up; is strongest when he is weakest; richest when he is poorest and happiest when he feels the worst. He dies so he can live; forsakes in order to have; gives away so he can keep; sees the invisible; hears the inaudible; and knows that which passeth knowledge.

A. W. Tozer

5
ALMOST CHRISTIANITY

I would like to buy $3 worth of God, please, not enough to explode my soul or disturb my sleep, but just enough to equal a cup of warm milk or a snooze in the sunshine. I don't want enough of Him to make me love a black man or pick beets with a migrant. I want ecstasy, not transformation; I want the warmth of the womb, not a new birth. I want a pound of the Eternal in a paper sack. I would like to buy $3 worth of God, please.

Wilbur Rees
$3.00 Worth of God

The only tragedy with the Christian faith is that it's never been tried.

attributed to George Bernard Shaw

GOD IS EAGER TO TEACH US through almost every event in our lives if we are but willing to listen. This was underlined in my life through an experience one Saturday morning. I had risen very early because I was in the process of training my dog, who was then less than a year old. I wanted to take her out before the traffic started, and she responded very well. The weeks and months of training seemed to have gotten through to her. She would sit or lie down both by verbal signals and hand signals. Likewise, though it was difficult for her, she would stay and then proceed in response to either verbal signals or hand signals.

I was quite pleased, until I realized that she still had difficulty in heeling. Out of her eagerness, or perhaps her protective instinct, she refused to walk with her ear next to my knee but insisted on getting ahead of me—first by a few inches, then by a few feet, and finally by a few dog's lengths if I didn't control it.

I tried everything that I thought might work. I tried slowing down. I would stop, and she would return to a heel position and sit down, but as soon as we started moving, she would sneak out ahead of me. For almost half an hour I tried working with her, using every technique I knew.

Finally my frustration level burst. Reaching down and grabbing her by the ears, I scolded her in my sternest voice: "Hey! No *almost* discipline this morning!"

As I stood up, I felt as if somebody were tapping me on the shoulder and saying the same thing to me.

We walked back towards the house. I began noticing how Schar's difficulty with her master was quite similar to the problems I have with my Master. It seems that I can obey certain commands better than others. But my biggest problem is in moving from one place to the next. Whether because of my eagerness or my lack of discipline, I've noticed that I, too, tend to stray ahead of the Master.

It was still quite early when we arrived back home. We sat on the porch together while I contemplated what this meant in my life. I was embarrassed at what I discovered.

I realized how many times I had been satisfied to come home in the evening, recognizing the impossibility of the task but somehow condoning my posture within it by saying, "I was *almost* your person today, Lord." I would pat myself on the back with the rationalization that I was at least better than some. Unknowingly, I had allowed my life to settle into what I now call "Almost Christianity." Because of the difficulty of the task, because of my fear of accountability to others, because of my defensiveness and unwillingness to live up to the demands of Scripture and of God himself, I had slowly and imperceptibly become very good at excusing myself.

Then I thought what it would have been like if Jesus had done the same thing. What if God had almost revealed himself in Jesus Christ? What if Christ were almost born and almost lived and almost died? What if he would have said, "Ask and it will almost be given you; seek and you will almost find; knock and it will almost be opened to you"? What if he would have said, "Come to me, all who labor and are heavy-laden, and I will almost give you rest"? And what if Jesus had told his disciples, "For whosoever would save his life will lose it, and whosoever loses his life for my sake will almost find it"?

My Almost Christianity took on a much different light. I realized how many times I had played the game of being one of Jesus' "almost disciples." I recalled how many times I had prayed almost believing and walked through my days as if he were almost risen.

It was not a question of theology. It was a question of life-style—whether or not I had a life-style that could match what I said I believed, whether or not, as some have said, I could walk my talk.

Harvard did a study some years ago on the subject of nonverbal communication, and I was stunned at its conclusion. The research revealed that there are over seven hundred thousand different ways to communicate without words. This knowledge must serve as a constant reminder that we don't just speak the message, we *are* the message. When we limit Christ's message to spoken words, we are not only limiting what he might do, but we are also placing ourselves under a tremendous handicap when we try to communicate it—ignoring seven hundred thousand ways, and using only one.

We may know the impact of our words. Rarely do we know the even more indelible impact of our life-style. Zacchaeus could not see Jesus, the Bible says, because the crowd was in the way. They were between him and Jesus, and he was not tall enough to see over them. I wonder if the same thing is not true today—if some who claim to know Christ are not in the way of others seeing the Master. Our bodies may not keep anybody from seeing Jesus, but our lives can and sometimes do. Sometimes people cannot see Jesus because our lives are in the way. They say, "If that is Christianity, I don't want it." What they have seen is usually Almost Christianity.

Fortunately, there are just as many stories on the other side of the ledger. "I have never seen Jesus, but I have seen Dr. Shephard," remarked a poor Armenian who had seen the Christlike service of that great medical missionary in the Near East.[1] Christ had lived there, incarnate in the life of one man.

It is important to remember that we are called to *be* his witnesses, not just to *do* witnessing for him (Acts 1:8). It's not a matter of imitation as much as it is inhabitation. The Sermon on the Mount doesn't command us to act salty, but to be the earth's salt. Salt creates thirst. Our life-styles need to continually create a thirst for the things of God in others. Our lives should be such that people would continually come to us and ask us to explain ourselves.

TO BE AND NOT TO DO

When God chose to reveal himself uniquely, he did it through a person, through a life-style—because he knew then, as now, that what we are is far more potent than what we say. Two thousand years ago God declared unambiguously in the life of Jesus Christ that human flesh is a good conductor of divine electricity—and, as far as I understand, he hasn't changed His mind.

The great problem with Jesus' message is not that it cannot be understood, but that it can. The difficulty is not one of which translation we read, but whether or not we can translate what we know into life-style.

Almost Christianity will reveal itself in countless subtle ways. I know many who claim that "with Christ *all* things are possible"—except to help them lose weight. I know those who extol the benefits of quiet time—but don't have enough time for contemplation themselves. Others lecture on the resurrection—and try to do everything on their own power. I know people who give sermons on the Lordship of Christ—but who can't slow down, because they think the world would collapse without their activities. Some people applaud the security we have in Christ—but are unwilling to take any chances. And still others glorify the freedom that is ours—but are still enslaved to their work.

Do not misunderstand; I am not proposing by any means a certain level of perfectionism, which has already been a source of a great deal of false hope in the body of Christ. We aren't simply to give up all activity in an effort to "surrender" ourselves to the Lord.

It is merely my contention that we are living in an age, not unlike other ages, that demands first of all a deep, quality relationship with Jesus Christ. This era's pace of life has changed so radically that it demands we take a solid look at our life-styles, including both work and leisure. We cannot afford to simply try to keep up with the new pace. But we must constantly remind ourselves that we are a part of the permanent, and that we are called to be holy, which means to be different and to have a distinct identity in Christ.

Alvin Toffler, among others, has been incisive in his diagnosis of our age. He says we live in a world of unprecedented change, eruption, and above all else, hurry. We live in a precooked, prepackaged, plastic-wrapped, instant society where relationships are increasingly temporary. "Future shock"—too much change in too short a time. We've come to look for instant intimacy, instant leisure, instant happiness. We develop simulated, artificial everything (including life-styles) in an effort to catch up with a world that is changing faster than we can cope with it. The result is experimentation, second-guessing, dissatisfaction, and overwhelming feelings of instability. The result is an attempt to "keep up," which forces us to increasing levels of superficiality. The problem is that most people don't recognize the way our hurry-up culture is shaping us.

If we do not truly understand the problem, then our solutions will be inadequate. And I believe that we will simply end up with other manifestations of Almost Christianity: Instant Christianity, Bionic Christianity, a commitment to the Kingdom of Niceness rather than the Kingdom of God. Or else we overcompensate and our commitment to Christ becomes our prison rather than one that frees us. We become Christian workaholics.

But we are called to *be* different. We are called to *be* his witnesses. As Lao-Tzu said, "The most important thing to do is to be." As the Psalmist said, "Be still and know that I am God."

My dog still struggles with heeling properly, and I still

struggle to have both my words and my life demonstrate that God can be trusted. But there is hope. The world, ultimately, is his responsibility. We are called to be faithful, not frantic. If we are to meet the challenges of today, there must be integrity between our words and our lives, and more reliance on the source of our purpose.

"Unless the Lord builds the house,
those who build it labor in vain.
Unless the Lord watches over the city,
the watchman stays awake in vain.
It is in vain that you rise up early
and go late to rest,
eating the bread of anxious toil;
for he gives to his beloved sleep."
Psalm 127:1-2

Almost Christianity reveals itself in feverish work, excessive hurry, and exhaustion. I believe that the Enemy has done an effective job of convincing us that unless a person is worn to a frazzle, running here and there, he or she cannot possibly be a dedicated, sacrificing, spiritual Christian. Perhaps the Seven Deadly Sins have recruited another member—Overwork.

We need to remember that our strength lies not in hurried efforts and ceaseless long hours, but in our quietness and confidence.

The world today says, "Enough is not enough."

Christ answers softly, "Enough is enough."

6
PLAY IS
A FEELING
TO BE LEARNED

Have the old pharisees and the new zealots, with their conservative and revolutionary legalism, scared us away from freedom, from joy and spontaneity? It is unlikely that anything good or just will come about unless it flows from an abundance of joy and the passion of love.

Jurgen Moltmann
The Theology of Play

WHEN WAS THE LAST TIME you woke up rested—I mean really rested and exuberant and excited about meeting the day?

When was the last time you kidnapped a friend, spontaneously, and took him or her out for an ice cream cone just to bring the surprise of joy into their life, and then found that the happiness that you were giving them got all over you, too?

When was the last time you had an experience so deeply joyous, so undefinably happy, that when you tried to explain it to someone else, there weren't enough words?

When was the last time you did something a little bit crazy—wore a top hat to a movie? Or brought flowers home just to celebrate Tuesday? Or hid secret love notes around the house for the kids or your spouse?

When was the last time you laughed until the tears poured from your eyes?

Or, do you insist on being one of those nice, dead people who continue to spend most of their time preparing to live? Do you even know what brings you deepest joy? Are your vacations only something that prepare you again for work? Or are they special times of loving and living, of learning and relaxing? Are you truly able to relax? Or are you still convinced of the notion that the world just might cave in if you dare stop for a while? When the psalmist said, "O taste and see that the Lord is good," was he in touch with reality or merely putting words on paper? If you were to paint a picture of the Christian life today from your perspective, what kinds of color would you use? Is life something to be celebrated or endured?

William James said that faith is either a dull habit or an acute fever. Which is it for you?

Do you have time to play? Do you know how to play?

Do you have time to rest? Do you even know what it means? Interestingly enough, Scripture not only calls us to enter into God's rest, but to live out of that rest. The temptation to overwork is potentially one of the greatest problems for dedicated, sincere Christians today. We are more often characterized by frantic activity, fatigue, and weariness than love, compassion, and joy.

"Elijah, in 1 Kings 18—19, is an excellent example of this problem . . . He was God's faithful prophet. He stood up against King Ahab, who repeatedly threatened and sought his life. Elijah offered his sacrifice to God upon an altar saturated with water, and God sent down fire upon

it to verify that he was the only true God and that Elijah
was his servant . . ..After such manifestations of God's
power and presence, a woman named Jezebel threatened
Elijah. He became afraid, fled, and sank into depression
so severe he wanted to die.

"What caused this depression? There were several
factors. For one thing, there had been a famine and
drought, and that may have weakened the prophet. Also
God had told Elijah to confront formidable King Ahab.
Instead Elijah imposed on a friend, Obadiah, to go ahead
of him to the king. We cannot determine from the Bible
whether or not this was in God's plan or whether the
manipulation sapped Elijah of some of his energy. We
find, also, that the prophet was totally unaware of many
others who loved and served God. He felt alone, saying,
"I, even I only, am left; and they seek my life" (1 Kings
19:14). And to top it all off, he forgot God's obvious
blessing upon him, the miracles performed by his own
hands. The last straw was being intimidated by the
queen.

"How many of these things, or others not recorded, led
up to his fatigue and depression? We don't know. We do
know, however, that God did not reprimand him for his
lack of faith. God's profound diagnosis was simple:
'Elijah, you need rest and food' (See 19:5-7). Then he
went, in the strength of the Lord . . . Though God had
business to do with Elijah, he had time to let him first eat
and rest . . . God could have given him instant nourish-
ment and refreshment, but he didn't . . . The supernatural power involved to perform miracles was abso-
lutely necessary to vindicate God's power before the
nonbelieving generation. But it wasn't in God's plan . . .
for Elijah's personal needs at this time, which were to be
met by the normal, natural, God-given means—food and
rest."[1]

A friend of mine once reminded me that the God of

Israel neither sleeps nor slumbers—but that doesn't mean we don't have to. Jesus frequently encouraged his friends to rest. "Let's get away from the crowds for a while and rest," said Jesus (Mark 6:31). For so many people were coming and going that they scarcely had time to eat.

I don't understand how the Master could take time to go alone into the desert to fast and pray when the whole world was starving and in chaos, when countless individuals needed him. He had a proven track record of healing. I just don't understand . . . but he did. I don't understand how he could continue to love and give when he was rejected like he was. And how he could respond rather than react. And how he could maintain his inner poise rather than project the pain. I don't understand how he could tell us not to worry about life when times are so difficult (Luke 12:22). I don't know how he could tell us that some of us are working too hard—that we're too busy, and that our busyness will actually cause us to miss the Kingdom of God (Luke 14:16-24). I don't understand how he could say that sometimes it is better just to sit at his feet than to be up doing things for him (Luke 10:38-42). Or how he could promise rest in the midst of a world filled with turmoil and distorted with pain (Matthew 11:28-30). Or how he could ask us to be like little children, when the world needs more firm leadership and harder workers (Matthew 19:13-15). I don't understand how Jesus could play and celebrate and enjoy life, when the world was in the condition it was in (Matthew 11:19). I don't understand . . . but he did.

And I am deeply thankful that truth is not dependent on me and my perceptions.

Are you controlling life more but enjoying it less? Does it seem sometimes that you're working longer and harder but the joy you seek is still one step ahead of you? Are the words *rest* and *play* becoming strangers? Or even worse, unattainable goals?

The inevitable question is "Why?" And how do we change? Some of the obstacles are obvious, some are quite subtle.

The first obstacle, as we have already mentioned, is a preoccupation with work. We have become so compulsively utilitarian that we can scarcely hear, see, or feel the world about us without having to attach a purpose to it. If we can't, at least at times, do something totally purposeless, perhaps it is because we do not really believe in the sovereignty of God. Possibly we're taking ourselves too seriously, placing too much importance on ourselves and the work we are doing. Yes, God works through people, but our work isn't the only reason God created us. We can trust God to continue his ultimate purposes for a little while even without our sweat.

> A purposeful purposelessness
> and purposeless play.
> This play, however, is an
> affirmation of life.
> Not an attempt to bring order out of chaos,
> not to suggest improvements in creation,
> but simply a way of waking up
> the very life we are living.
> —John Cage[2]

Another problem is that we have not given play and rest a proper dignity. We still have the conviction that the idle mind is the devil's workshop. We still house a subconscious guilt that if we enjoy life too much, something must be wrong. And yet, when we play, we truly say yes to God and yes to life. We need to remember that 2 Corinthians 1:19-20 tells us that Christ is the eternal Yes.

And finally, one of the chief obstacles is our unconscious desire to constantly compare. Our subconscious perfectionism has been subtly but indelibly planted on our brains. The media, especially advertisers, have two consistent and dominant messages. The first is that "you are not OK!" In order to convince you to buy their product, every manufacturer must persuade you that you are not yet complete, that you lack something you need to be happy, i.e. their product. The second message is that you must never be satisfied—compare, compare, compare. Products cannot be just different; one must be superior.

Much of the time, I have the distinct feeling that my life has not yet started, and I'm still waiting for the proper moment to begin. Yet unless we are able to live fully in the present, the future will always be a disappointment. Each day is a new, unrepeatable, once-in-a-lifetime gift. To waste it by always waiting for tomorrow, by continually preparing to live, or by thinking that enough is never enough, is pure folly.

A young Jewish girl, surrounded by the horrors of a Nazi concentration camp, had the grace and composure to write the following poem. Her words have seared themselves into my mind because I recognize how often I lack the gratitude and maturity she must have had.

> From tomorrow on
>   I shall be sad
> From tomorrow on—
>   not today.
> Today I will be glad,
>   and every day
>   no matter how bitter it may be
>   I shall say

ENOUGH IS ENOUGH

> From tomorrow on I shall be sad
> not today.

I get slightly embarrassed when I read this poem and then look at the cellophaned unhappiness that surrounds me. For although we live in the wealthiest nation in the world, during a time of relative peace, in an age of overwhelming opportunity, we have written a less grateful adaptation of the above poem, which goes like this:

> From tomorrow on I shall be happy,
> From tomorrow on.
> Not today.
> And every day, no matter how good things may be,
> I shall say
> from tomorrow on I'll be happy
> not today.

One of the most important principles of quality leisure is focusing on what we have rather than on what we don't. A close friend of mine once beautifully defined peace as "the absence of envy." It is in the absence of comparison, the absence of all the walls we so needlessly put up— between me and you, rich and poor, life and death, work and play. It is being able to live unconditionally, in the complete freedom God has given us.

Is it so small a thing to have enjoyed the sun, to have loved, to have laughed, to have lived? Is it so small a thing to enjoy our days and to enjoy God and to enjoy being who we are? Is it so small a thing to be grateful and to be happy, to be at peace with ourselves and with God? Is it so small a thing to feel fit and energetic and free and wonderfully alive? Is it so small a thing to fly a kite with your child, to take a walk, to play catch, to wrestle on the lawn, to tickle and be tickled until your laughter can't be controlled? Is it so small a thing to make our days count rather than count our days?

Play is more than just nonwork. It is one of the pieces in the puzzle of our existence, a place for our excesses and exuberances. It is where life lives in a very special way. It is the time when we forget our problems for a while and remember who we are. Play is more than just a game. It is where you recognize again the supreme importance of life itself. Like a child, you see life as it is and as it was meant to be. In play you can abandon yourself, you can immerse yourself without restraint, you can pierce life's complexities and confusions. You can be whole again without trying.

Play reminds me I am a body. I know, by experience, that, like David, I am fearfully and wondrously made. I know from my reading that I have approximately 263 bones and 600 muscles. A scientist can inform me that I am a microcosm of the universe, containing 92 elements of the cosmos in my body. But play tells me that I am a living miracle, that I am not ordinary, that I am by creation more marvelous than all the statistics ever compiled and categorized. Play hints at all the hidden possibilities that invite me to come be discovered. As George Sheehan points out, "There are those who, like Freud, claim that the two main goals in life are love and work. What they fail to see is the primacy of play. Before love, before work, there was play. . . . Play is a taste of the Paradise from which we came, a foretaste of the Paradise we will enter."

Is it so small a thing to rediscover play, to participate passionately in some activity for its own intrinsic value? To transcend reason and logic for a while, to experience work as more than labor and religion as more than rules? Is it so small a thing to take time to remember, to blow out candles on a birthday cake, to celebrate a friendship, or a

ENOUGH IS ENOUGH

lifetime? To take time to read, to listen, or to dream, to let your mind and heart be quiet for a while? Is it so small a thing to feel part of this earth and its peoples, to feel part of its purpose and plan? Is it so small a thing to stop and hear God's words to us, and begin anew from wherever we are?

Leisure—giving yourself permission to get involved in life—can become:

the path of blessing
the hope of peace
the hinge of praise.

Leisure can become the time in your life when you can say, and believe, that enough is more than enough.

Part 3
Enough Is More than Enough

The glory of God is man fully alive.

Saint Irenaeus

7

THE TIME
OF OUR LIVES

I wasted an hour one morning beside a mountain stream,
I seized a cloud from the sky above and fashioned myself a dream,
In the hush of the early twilight, far from the haunts of men,
I wasted a summer evening, and fashioned my dream again.
Wasted? Perhaps. Folks say so who never have walked with God,
When lanes are purple with lilacs or yellow with goldenrod.
But I have found strength for my labors in that one short evening
  hour.
I have found joy and contentment; I have found peace and
  power.
My dreaming has left me a treasure, a hope that is strong and
  true.
From wasted hours I have built my life and found my faith anew.

Author unknown

I ONCE READ A THOUGHT-PROVOKING article entitled, "If You Are 35, You Have 500 Days to Live."[1] Its thesis was that when you subtract the time spent sleeping, working, tending to personal matters, hygiene, odd chores, medical matters, eating, traveling, and miscellaneous time-stealers, in the next thirty-six years you will have roughly the equivalent of only five hundred days left to spend as you wish. No wonder the Psalmist advised, "So teach us to number our days that we may apply our hearts to wisdom."

It is for this reason that we need new attitudes. We need new principles and new skills to help involve us more deeply in the time God has given us. We need leisure. God has set before us an adventure like no other. If we are willing to enter this journey of faith with openness, intelligence, and enthusiasm, we may discover dimensions of life we had never before dreamed of.

In leisure the mind is liberated from the immediate, the usual, the necessary problems, to meditate on ultimate matters. Through leisure we are given permission to develop a new perspective on life. Through leisure we may come to better understand the wonder of being alive and to take time to share it with those we love.

In this chapter and those that follow, we will begin to offer some practical suggestions for redirecting our lives. First, we'll present some general principles, and in the final chapters, we'll show some specific things you might want to try. Before we can do that, we must understand something about time.

For a Christian there is no such thing as "free time." All of the Christian's time is redeemed and belongs to the one who has set us free. Therefore, it is impossible for a committed believer to say his working time is more valuable than his leisure time.

Second, all of us are given exactly the same amount of time each day—24 hours, or 1,440 minutes, or 86,400 seconds. No matter how you look at it, it's the same for each of us. The difference lies, however, in how each of us deals with it. We all put our own unique stamp upon our time. Each of us has both different purposes and different capacities for it, but that's part of the magic of being alive. And in God's eyes, none of us are more important than another. He made each one of us special, one-of-a-kind human beings.

Because each of us is called to weave his own unique tapestry of time and talent, and because of God's immense love, we must take the gift of time and use it to his best advantage.

As we move closer to God's rhythm for our lives, we realize that he has given us exactly enough time to achieve his purpose for us.

Therefore, one of the first principles we must deal with is to not be vague with our lives and God's time but to "freely decide to create the mood of the day, rather than let the circumstances and conditions of the day rule my life. With my spirit (the breath of God in me) I will transform the raw matter of my life and make it beautiful. This is my purpose. This is my hope. This is an adventure like no other."[2]

What would you do if every morning your bank phoned, informing you that your account had been credited in the amount of 86,400 pennies ($864)—but with the stipulation that it had to be spent that very day? No balance could be carried over to the next day. Every evening canceled whatever sum you failed to use. Think about what you could do with such a gift. You would probably draw out and use every cent every day.

Leslie Flynn, in his book *It's About Time,* says that we do have such a bank—called the First World Bank of Time. Every morning this bank credits your account with 86,400 seconds—but no balances are carried into the next day. Every night erases what you fail to use. Failure to draw it out and use its treasure is your loss. No previous day's time can be reclaimed.[3]

ENOUGH IS MORE THAN ENOUGH

I went out Lord,
    men were coming and going,
    walking and running.
In spite of all their grand efforts,
    they were still short of time.
Lord, you must have made a mistake in your
calculation.

Lord, I have time.
I have plenty of time, all the time that you give me,
    the years of my life,
        the days of my years,
            the hours of my days.
Mine to fill quietly, calmly,
Up to the brim.

Michel Quoist[4]

Man lives in three tenses: past, present, and future. The day is the smallest division of God-given time. Seconds, minutes, and hours are artificial and man-made, but the day is a product of creation—a span of time God has provided.

Every morning brings new mercies and blessings. Said the Psalmist, "Blessed be the Lord who daily bears us up" (Ps. 68:19). Jeremiah said, "The steadfast love of the Lord never ceases, his mercies never come to an end; they are new every morning; great is thy faithfulness" (Lam. 3:22-23).

A saintly invalid, who was crippled and had to spend the rest of her life in bed, was once asked, "How long must you lie like that?"

She answered, "Just one day at a time." Divine help is never promised for a month or even a week in advance, but only for each day—"as your days, so shall your strength be" (Deut. 33:25).

The New Testament uses two different words to describe time. We need to be aware of the different meanings if we are to learn God's rhythm for our lives.

Chronos is time governed by the clock. *Kairos,* on the other hand, is measured by events or special moments. *Chronos* is timetables and prearranged work schedules. *Kairos* is the rhythm of planting and harvest, energy and fatigue, that encourages human action to break forth in the time of ripeness.

The difference between *chronos* and *kairos* might well be illustrated by what just happened to me while I was writing this. *Chronos* says that the book is due in a few weeks and that I must be very disciplined about my time. *Kairos* says that my sons just came in the door and nothing is more important than that. *Chronos* says I have an outline I'm trying to follow and a time schedule that must be met today. *Kairos* says some things are more important than outlines—like my sons inviting me to go for a walk.

We took the walk.

Mark Twain once said, "To get the full value of joy you must have somebody to divide it with." My joy was just divided and multiplied in geometric proportions by the walk with my two sons.

It had stormed all afternoon, the rain pounding on the windows and leaving big puddles for the guys to walk through as we strolled along. Moisture was still seeping out of the fence and dripping down the windowpane. The trees were still shedding tears of joy and the earth's laughter. Spectacular clouds danced with the sun, and the three of us stopped time. We didn't walk very far, but that didn't matter. It didn't even really make any difference where we went. The point was that we went together . . . Zachary leaping and jumping from puddle to puddle in his boots that his "Nana and PopPop" (his grandparents) had sent him from a thrift shop . . . Joshua waddling and weaving as only a one-year-old can. Clothed in his older brother's old coat, which hangs down past his fingertips, and in a hat perched cockeyed over his eyebrows, and in shoes so small that they look like toys, he weaved his way down the sidewalk in front of me. Our dog, Schar, ran back and forth between them. In the moist, crisp air you could see her breath floating up. The sunlight bounced off prisms of water on cyclone fences and leaves of grass. We had time, or I should say, took time, to enjoy these things. Zachary picked up pinecones to bring home to his mom and stuffed my pockets until they were bulging over. Joshua stopped and stood precariously at the edge of a curb to listen to the water gurgle down into a sewer, squealing with delight at this little city river. Schar barked and chased sounds and shadows. And we said hi to neighbors and wished them well.

Little things, like the bird that sang to the sunset, took on a new kind of magnitude. For a few moments our laughter seemed as important as the Middle East situation, or maybe even more. I forgot what *chronos* it was. It didn't seem too important now. The only things that seemed to matter were here and now and us. The earth turned a few more degrees and the sun gently nibbled away at the horizon and then disappeared. We became silhouettes playing hopscotch on the playground— dancing on the white lines that were a little harder to see, Zachary running ahead and Joshua trying to follow his voice. I was aware of my breath as it misted in front of me. I was aware of how tiny and fragile my children were. I looked across the playground at Joshua, only a few feet high, and he seemed like a colorful little dot in an immense universe, an immense playground, which no one will ever fully understand.

Then he turned and giggled and ran toward me with his arms outstretched. Only a father can fully know how that feels. Once again my life took on a meaning beyond time. *Kairos*—wrapped in an eloquence and a simplicity that can only be experienced briefly and remembered always.

We held hands as we walked home in the dark. And we shook the branches of trees so that they would sprinkle their drops on top of us. And we laughed. For a moment we filled the universe with our joy and I wanted that short walk home to last even longer. But I suppose the beauty of those kind of moments lies in the fact that you can't hold on to them. *Kairos,* where all things seem possible, where past, present, and future seem to melt into oneness and hope. *Kairos,* where we again stop long enough to let life love us.

8
MIDGET GURUS
OF PLAY

I want to be doing things to be doing them . . .
I don't want to do nice things for people so that I will be "nice."
I don't want to work to make money,
I want to work to work.
Today I don't want to live for,
I want to live.

Hugh Prather
Notes to Myself

GURUS TEACH PEOPLE PROFOUND TRUTHS—at least
that's how it is supposed to work. What we don't realize is
that we don't have to go chasing around the world to find
gurus with the secret to happiness. Most of us have some
of the finest gurus in the world in our own homes, and we
don't even know it.

I happen to have two live-in, pint-sized gurus who have
taught me more about life than all the books I've ever
read. Their names are Zachary and Joshua (you met
them in the last chapter), and they prefer to give away
their unadorned wisdom rather than market it. They

give most when they are unaware of it. It just happens—they live their message—relaxed, flexible, and unpretentious.

There is no separation between their minds and their bodies. They have the unconscious unity that people spend years and fortunes to find. Their emotions are fully expressed—nothing is held back. When they are hungry, they eat. When tired, they sleep. And when the wind wakes up, so do they.

I've seen the wind play in their hair and dance at their feet. They greet it like a friend and giggle at its caresses. These tiny little brothers of the wind and sea cannot wait to be outside—surrounded, enveloped, enlivened by this kinship. I've watched them enjoy the elemental stuff of life—earth, wind, and water. I've seen the surpassing joy of them hugging the earth and chasing the wind and trying to catch it with their tiny hands. And sometimes the wind, like a gentle playmate, turns and chases them back amid wild laughter and scampering. Oh, Lord, what has happened to our rigid bodies and hearts when the wind no longer tickles us?

Their uncanny ability to immerse themselves completely in what they are doing is a living lesson for all of us. One day they were playing outside with some of their friends. They were enacting all of their heroes—Superman, Green Hornet, Spiderman, Batman, and the like. Each was getting his part, when Zac looked over to me and asked a central question regarding his hero. "Is he the one that flies, dad?" When I said yes, he cheered with exuberance: "I'm the one who flies! I'm the one who flies!"

As a father I not only shared his excitement—for I'm glad my son wants to fly—but I also thought of the many times I've grounded myself by simply not appropriating some of the promises given to me. As Paul said, "We are sons of freedom. Christ has set us free, and we are called to stay free." We, too, were made for flying.

Research, I understand, has "proven scientifically" that it is impossible for the bumblebee to fly. Based on factors of body size, density, shape, weight, wingspan, and speed of the wings, it is aeronautically impossible for this creature to get off the ground. However, someone forgot to notify the bumblebee. What we need is enough self-forgetfulness, enough abandonment, enough audacity to do the same. What we need are more Christian bumblebees.

I met a man once who impressed me so much with his awareness that I asked him, "How did you ever learn so much?"

He replied simply, "I watched children—carefully, observantly, diligently, and often."

Children have so much to teach us. They are such natural models for what we seek to know. They contain, without knowing it, a knowledge that could match volumes of books or years of college. One evening not too long ago, I sat and watched Joshua (then fourteen months old) play in the kitchen. He had been sleeping, and I was reading. He woke up, and I thought my work would be interrupted. He didn't bother me, but watching him, I soon discovered that he had far more to teach me than the book I was reading. Some of the principles my midget gurus have taught me are:

● *Total immersion.* No matter what he's doing, he is not superficially involved. Whether he's throwing a ball, laughing, running, drawing, pulling pots and pans out of the cupboard, pushing a toy truck, or teasing our dog, he does it with his whole self, sans inhibitions.

● *Total concentration.* His mind is on one thing at a time and one thing only. It is interesting to note that the word *worry* comes from the Greek word *merimnao,* which is a combination of the two words *merizo,* meaning "to divide," and *nous,* meaning "mind" (including the faculties of perceiving, understanding, feeling, judging, determining). Hence, worry means "to divide the mind," or to be double-minded. Watch your children, especially the younger ones, and you will notice how free they are from this problem that plagues our society.

• *New perspectives.* I vividly remember a joyous incident that occurred just after I got home from the hospital. Zac was so glad to have me home that he tucked me into my chair at the breakfast table. Food was served, and our tradition has always been to return thanks before eating. Zac, being about 2½ at the time, was excited this particular morning to tell me that he'd learned to pray while I was gone, and asked if he could do so. I was delighted. His mother had taught him, "Jesus loves me, this I know . . ." but it didn't quite come out that way. He grabbed our hands, bowed his head, and began: "Jesus loves me—this our toast."

He was barely finished with breakfast when he was off for his morning "leisure," catching cups of sunshine in the doorway with his hands, laughing at the slightest nudge, being Casey Jones, and sharing how he's learned to say "cris-an-um-thum" to describe the flowers I'd received in the hospital. I noticed that his focus was always singular, on just what he was doing at the time. When he played with "bat bear," he *was* his pilot. Throughout the morning he became a dog trainer, Mr. Fix-it, a rock climber, and a singer—to name a few.

I loved it, and thought how different his perspective often is. It's real, down to earth, fresh, innocent, and un-*adult*-erated.

• *Ability to bounce back.* With children, only their bodies are small. Their curiosity fills entire rooms. Their energy comes in gigantic proportions, and their spirit is indomitable. When Zac was younger, he climbed some stairs only to tumble back down the full length. That didn't surprise me as much as what happened a few minutes later. The tears were barely dry when he was back at the bottom, ready to climb again. I remember wishing that evening that I could display such tenacity in so natural a manner, with such lack of fear of failure.

• *Total honesty and expression.* I admire how Joshua is so complete and open and honest with his feelings. When he is happy, he is laughter. When he is frustrated, his anger is undiluted, and he is sadness incarnate when he cries.

His wonderful sense of spontaneity shows him that nothing is "normal." A plastic bowl can become a hat. A sheet can become a tent or a hiding place or a boat. A broom becomes a horse to ride. The magic isn't necessarily coming from the things around him, but from within him. Curiosity reigns. Life is a constant question mark (or exclamation point!). Joshua tries to figure out how one pan goes inside another, how a door latch opens, what makes certain noises. His older brother tries to figure out how a clock ticks, a pen writes, and a pencil sharpener works. Everything contains the possibility of magical aliveness because of this imagination.

In a sense, they are both making life happen and letting life happen. Laughter doesn't have to be taught at this age. Play doesn't have to be justified. And rest is a natural part of their life-style. Every day I realize more and more that we have something to learn from these tiny little encyclopedias of life.

They have taught me of wonder and uninhibitedness, of gratitude and spontaneity, of unimpeded trust and freedom to change, of imagination and creativity. They have taught me to see everything as if it were for the first time and to share as if there were no end. They have taught me how to smell again, and taste, and touch. They have taught me about security, and why God calls us to be like little children.

9

FOUR COMMANDMENTS OF CONTENTMENT

Many people spend their entire life indefinitely preparing to live.
Paul Tournier
The Adventure of Living

HOW MANY TRULY CONTENT PEOPLE do you know? If you answer like most people, my second question will be "Why are there so few?"

Probably for a number of reasons. One, as we have already mentioned, is that many of us spend too much time practicing being unhappy. Two, we do not accept the real meaning of leisure and give ourselves permission to enjoy life. Three, we don't spend enough time and energy practicing being happy.

The apostle Paul said, "I have *learned* to be content, whatever the circumstances may be" (Phil. 4:11). For years I read that section of Scripture in wonder and awe of this saint who had this gift of being able to be content amid difficulties. I didn't realize, until one of my students pointed it out to me with a question, that this was not a natural, easy gift for Paul. It was a trait he developed through diligence and practice. He realized that, like every good thing, contentment takes practice and determination.

Here are four commandments that help develop contentment.

THOU SHALT LIVE HERE AND NOW

People have a tendency to cherish their dreams but rarely act to make them happen. So they continually look to the future for happiness, and their provisional lives right now are filled only with anticipation.

What we need to constantly emphasize is that life, God's life within us, is happening here and now, and the paradox is that we must practice the presence— otherwise it will elude us. My son said it so well one day when he said, "It's better here, isn't it, daddy?" We need to remind each other often that it is better here, and it is better now.

We are sitting on a miracle, but we don't recognize it—God has given us *everything* we need to be happy.

In an attempt to understand the incredible depth of Scripture and to be able to put hands and feet on it, I have begun a fifty-year commitment to understand one simple line in Scripture. It began a year and a half ago when I was hiking in the Sierras with Jack Meyer, a close friend of mine. We were discussing the promises of God that are available to us here and now. The verse that kept coming back to my mind was one that is probably repeated more and understood less than any other verse in Scripture. Our children learn it very early, and thus it becomes so familiar that it loses its impact. But it holds tremendous meaning—"The Lord is my Shepherd, I shall not want." Another version says, "The Lord is my Shepherd, therefore I lack nothing."

I realized that day how little I understood the real meaning of those words. And so I began a journey that taught me more about the power of God's promises than I ever would have dreamed of. Because he is my Lord and Shepherd, I lack nothing. And because of that, I have *everything* I need to be happy here and now.

A friend of mine shared a letter with me that he had received from his parents during a time of particular struggle.

"We have an idea," they wrote, "that God is leading us to a desired goal—he is not. His purpose is that I depend on him and his power now. If I can stay in the middle of the turmoil, calm and unperplexed, that is the end of God's purpose. God's training is for now. This minute. Not something in the future. God's end is to enable me to see that he can walk on the chaos of my life just now. If we have a further end in view, we do not pay sufficient attention to the immediate. When we realize obedience is the end, then each moment is precious. God never gives strength for tomorrow or the next hour, but only for the strain of the minute."

It helped me realize again that the peace and happiness we seek must begin with an unadorned acceptance of where we are and who we are. God is not only the God of history and of the future, but also very much the God of the now, the God of the process.

Avoiding the present moment has almost become a habit in our society. For the major part of our working lives we are taught to sacrifice the present for the future. When the future arrives, it becomes the present, and we must use it to prepare for the future. If this is lived out to its logical conclusion, we avoid enjoyment not only now but forever.

Avoid the temptation of wishing, hoping, and regretting—the most common tactics for evading the present. Abstain from the ritual of idealizing the future, which leads only to disappointment.

Invest in the present. The right time is any time. The best time is now. It is not necessary to surrender tomorrow or next year, but abandon yourself to God's presence and his will as it unfolds in your life moment to moment.

Live in the here and now. No matter who you are, or in what wealth or poverty you live, life will not allow you more than one minute at a time. What a blow to our ego—what hope for our souls.

THOU SHALT NOT HURRY

One Saturday morning a couple of years ago, I got caught hurrying again. I was on my way to coach our college football team. As usual, I'd tried to cram too much into the early morning hours. The car that made me pull over had a light that kept winking at me. A somber man in blue came toward me. The spaghetti-like inscriptions on his uniform indicated that he worked for Los Angeles County. He took his job very seriously. He gave me a copy of the yellow form he wrote to the municipal traffic court. The charge: I had broken the law. I was hurrying too fast.

On my way to the game I talked to the Lord about my predicament—or, to be more honest, he talked to me. He spoke; I listened. *You broke the law.* I agreed. It was hard not to, with that silly piece of paper in my hand. *No,* he continued, *you still don't understand. You broke The Law.*

ENOUGH IS MORE THAN ENOUGH

The worst part was not breaking an external, man-made law—although that is serious enough in itself—but in breaking a far greater, eternal rhythm. I had submitted to the sin of hurry.

Nikos Kazantzakis in his book, *Zorba the Greek*, relates a very simple but poignant event that shaped much of his thought and participation in time. "I remembered one morning when I discovered a cocoon in the bark of a tree, just as the butterfly was making a hole in its case and preparing to come out. I waited a while, but it was too long appearing and I was impatient. I bent over it and breathed on it to warm it. I warmed it as quickly as I could and the miracle began to happen before my eyes faster than life. The case opened. The butterfly started slowly crawling out and I shall never forget my horror when I saw how its wings were folded back and crumpled; the wretched butterfly tried with its whole trembling body to unfold them. Bending over it I tried to help it with my breath, in vain. It needed to be hatched out patiently. And the unfolding of the wings should be a gradual process in the sun. Now it was too late. My breath had forced the butterfly to appear all crumpled before its time. It struggled desperately and a few seconds later died in the palm of my hand.

"That little body is, I do believe, the greatest weight I have on my conscience. For I realized today that it is a mortal sin to violate the great laws of nature. We should not hurry. We should not be impatient. But we should confidently obey the eternal rhythm. If only that little butterfly could always flutter before me to show me the way."[1]

Our world seems intoxicated with hurry. It seems to be inundated with a hurricane desire to precipitate the future. One of the greatest sins of this age may be hurry. For in our impatient desire to make things happen, we have, inadvertently, overlooked what was really important.

Small wonder, then, that we have lost the ability to immerse ourselves in the simple delights of the earth—the wind against our faces, savory aromas in our nostrils, moist grass beneath our feet, a child in our arms. In our hurry to be someplace other than where we are, to be someone other than who we are, we have lost the ability to wonder.

As Jose Ortega Gasset said, "To be surprised, to wonder, is to begin to understand."[2]

Some men named Matthew, Mark, Luke, and John tried to tell us of a man who left eternity and entered into time, and yet who walked within the boundaries of an eternal rhythm. They tried to tell us of the love that was beyond measure; a hope beyond reason; and a life-style that could have its source in an eternal rhythm. We have been told that this rhythm, this peace, this love, this joy can, in fact, be ours. Little did they know, these men, these Gospel writers, how busy we would be. Little did they know how important our work would be. Little did they know about our important schedules and deadlines. But they told us about a life, the Life, who lived according to a different timetable. Even in our day, the eternal beat goes on.

THOU SHALT NOT TAKE THYSELF TOO SERIOUSLY

Things were going pretty badly for a certain British shipping line, and one of Sir John's colleagues was in his office filling the air with gloom. Sir John said to him sharply, "You've forgotten Rule Number Four."

His colleague responded with surprise, "What's Rule Number Four?"

"Rule Number Four," said Sir John, "is 'Don't take yourself too seriously.' "

"What are the other rules?"

"There aren't any others," Sir John replied.

One of the great problems these days is that we spend half our life developing a fine reputation and then the rest of our life being tyrannized by it. But which would you rather have—a Christian reputation or Jesus Christ? Jesus often reminds us to be childlike. He also reminded the Pharisees, in a somewhat less than tender posture, that they took themselves too seriously.

"For everyone who makes himself important will become insignificant, while the man who makes himself insignificant, will find himself important" (Luke 14:11).

"Then he gave this illustration to certain people who were confident of their own goodness and looked down on others: 'Two men went up to the Temple to pray, one was a Pharisee, the other was a tax collector. The Pharisee stood and prayed like this with himself, "Oh, God I do thank thee that I am not like the rest of mankind, greedy, dishonest, impure, or even like that tax collector over there. I fast twice every week; I give away a tenth part of all my income." But the tax collector stood in a distant corner, scarcely daring to look up to Heaven, and with a gesture of despair, said, "God, have mercy on a sinner like me." I assure you that he was the man who went home justified in God's sight rather than the other one. For everyone who sets himself up as somebody will become a nobody. And the man who makes himself a nobody will become somebody' " (Luke 18:9-14).

One of the greatest obstacles I wrestle with is that of taking myself too seriously. The result is a pretentious, defensive, brittle man who works five times harder than he needs to in order to continually prove himself to the world, and who forgets to laugh—especially at himself. The problems with taking ourselves too seriously are countless. Afraid to fail, we no longer risk. Afraid that someone will see behind our image, we no longer share. Afraid that we will appear to need help, we can no longer be vulnerable. Afraid to appear not religious enough to some, we no longer can confess. We withdraw into a petty world consumed in emptiness and fear, covered with the thick shell, worshiping an impotent God. The tragic result of taking ourselves too seriously is that in our fear of becoming childlike, in our fear of becoming a fool for Christ, in our fear of being seen as we are, we discover all too late that it's impossible to be fully human and fully alive.

This struggle became so real for me that I have found I need constant reminders to help me be free in Jesus Christ and not to take myself too seriously. So I carry small toys—a tiny Snoopy, or King Kong, or little squatty hippo, or any such object that I can get into my pocket. Those who know me well know that they're in the pockets of most of my coats and virtually all of my trousers. They sit on my desk, and they are by my books. They serve as a constant reminder not only of my children and how much I love them, but that I too am a child of God, and that he loves me, and I don't have to waste time taking myself too seriously.

"Eccentricity has always abounded when and where strength of character has abounded; and the amount of eccentricity in society has always been proportioned to the amount of genius, mental vigor and moral courage which it contained. That so few men now dare to be eccentric marks the chief danger of our time." (John Steward Mill)

ENOUGH IS MORE THAN ENOUGH

> If we are "mad" it is for God's glory. (2 Cor. 5:13)

"Plainly God's purpose was that your faith should rest not upon man's cleverness but upon the power of God" (1 Cor. 2:5).

"I have cheerfully made up my mind to be proud of my weaknesses, because they mean a deeper experience of the power of Christ. I can even enjoy my weaknesses, suffering, privations, persecutions and difficulties for Christ's sake. For my very weakness makes me strong in him" (2 Cor. 12:9-10).

THOU SHALT BE GRATEFUL

Someone once said, "Success is getting what you want. Happiness is wanting what you get." The Bible expresses the same idea a different way—"Give thanks in all circumstances; for this is the will of God in Christ Jesus for you" (1 Thess. 5:18, RSV).

The point is, the essence of happiness and peace lies in gratitude. "Delight yourselves in the Lord; yes, find your joy in him at all times . . . tell God every detail of your needs in earnest and thankful prayer, and the peace of God, which transcends human understanding, will keep constant guard over your hearts and minds as they *rest* in Christ Jesus" (Phil. 4:4-7).

Two things should be noted: (1) gratitude is not an option for a Christian, and (2) gratitude is the source of peace. We are not required to understand the process before we can employ it.

Possibly the greatest principle of leisure I know is the principle of insistent, consistent, persistent gratitude. If you would really like to change the world within you and thereby around you, learn to be diligent in thanksgiving.

One of our problems is that we attempt to express our gratitude in words only. Gratitude can be expressed by hard work, by patience, by laughter, by creativity, by persistence, by the quality of your love, by the depth of your hope, and by the certainty of your peace. Gratitude has no substitute. It's the surest way I know to emotional and spiritual health.

"I asked God for strength that I might achieve.
I was made weak that I might learn humbly to obey.

I asked God for health that I might do greater things.
I was given infirmity that I might do better things.

I asked for riches that I might be happy.
I was given poverty that I might be wise.

I asked for power that I might have the praise of men.
I was given weakness that I might feel the need of God.

I asked for all things that I might enjoy life.
I was given life that I might enjoy all things.

I got nothing that I asked for
but everything I had hoped for . . .

Almost despite myself my unspoken prayers were answered.

I am among all men most richly blessed."

Unknown Confederate Soldier

10
MAKE LIFE HAPPEN

It was no ordinary joy; it was a sublime, absurd, and unjustifiable gladness. Not only unjustifiable, contrary to all justification.

Nikos Kazantzakis
Zorba the Greek

He is most fatigued who knows not what to do.

N. Boileau

WITHIN EACH OF US LIES THE FREEDOM to be different, the capacity to be happy. But the process demands both grace and discipline. The need to bring together these two apparently opposing forces has led me to sculpt two concepts.

The first emphasizes our ability to change our circumstances, to influence our environment, to alter our affairs. It requires creative, graceful effort. It demands courage to avoid being controlled by circumstances, to create a new pattern that will be a catalyst for joy. I call

90

this process "graceful discipline"—making life happen. The second concept focuses on our capacity to enjoy, and on our ability to change our attitude when we can't change the circumstances. It requires the power of the Holy Spirit to transcend the situation, to create an inner environment that supersedes the external one. As Victor Frankl concluded after his experience in a Nazi concentration camp, "They could take everything from me except one thing—and that was the attitude with which I chose to respond to the situation."[1] I call this concept "disciplined grace"—letting life happen.

When both of these processes are used, the doors swing open, and truly abundant life begins. In this chapter, we will concentrate on graceful discipline. In the next chapter, we'll focus on disciplined grace.

GRACEFUL DISCIPLINE

One of the interesting and ironic principles of quality leisure is that it often takes hard work, discipline, and effort. If you want to live life to the maximum, you must learn how to arise early and seize the day, to get the jump on it before it gets the jump on you, to immerse yourself in the heart of life rather than remaining on the periphery, insulated from any consequences. On the wall of a college workout room, I saw this statement: "A person who says he can't and a person who says he can are, strangely enough, usually both right."

God wants you to do more than merely exist. You must live—and that means to the fullest. It requires that you must do more than simply look. It means you must observe with feeling, with involvement, and participation. It requires that you do more than simply think; you must discipline yourself to take time to ponder, to contemplate, and to respond. And it requires that you do more than simply talk; you must say something (and that means you must live a life that gives you enough substance that you have something to say). Someone once said, "The pessimist sees the difficulty in every opportunity; the optimist sees the opportunity in every difficulty." The famous comic strip philosopher Pogo once said, "Gentlemen, we are surrounded by insurmountable opportunities."

Making life happen means such things as: *making time* to think, for it is the source of power; *making time* to play, because it is the source of freedom, spontaneity, relaxation, and the secret of youth. It is also *making time* to read, for that is the foundation of knowledge. It is *making time* to worship, for that is the pathway of blessing, and washes the dust of earth from our eyes. It is *making time* to help and enjoy friends, for there is no other happiness that can match this. It is *making time* to love, for if you don't, it will fade away, and the greatest sacrament of life will be lost. It is *making time* to laugh and pray, for those are the two things that lighten life's loads.

It means allowing God to help you make sufficient time available to be with your family. This will not happen without deliberate planning and possible sacrifice.

Likewise, we must *make time* to be alone with God, which is not only the greatest privilege of life, but the source of everything else we do.

One of the greatest sins a Christian can commit against God, against the Holy Spirit, and against his fellowman is the sin of unreached potential. "Every one to whom much is given, of him will much be required," the Bible says (Luke 12:48). Unreached potential means not disciplining ourselves enough to become who we were created to be. It means that we allow our patterns of life to become frozen, and our achievements have such low ceilings that we allow ourselves the comfort of convenience. And in our lack of ambition, we perish.

What can we do? Obviously the issue is complex, and there are no easy solutions. But the first thing we need is *graceful discipline.* Graceful because it needs to be nourished consistently and directed by the Holy Spirit. It needs to become habitual enough that it does not always require a gnashing of teeth; instead, it soon becomes an effortless kind of discipline, a natural, fluid, determined energy that is aimed at precise goals. It will, in a sense, be a discipline out of rest.

How do we begin to discover our potentiality? Here are at least a few practical suggestions.

FIRST THINGS FIRST

Essential to actualizing our potential, whether in work or leisure, is to be rightly related to God. Nothing can replace the power of an unambiguous, personal relationship with Jesus Christ. It has power that no program or idea will ever begin to touch. The Christian life is not imitation, but habitation. Christ in you is a continuous gift. Peace with God, peace with each other, and peace with ourselves all come in the same package.

The two key words to remember are:

Justification: God accepts me as I am.

I do not have to reform, improve my figure, or anything else to come to Christ. He starts with me where I am.

Sanctification: God accepts me as I can be.

Once we are justified, we are free to change—and change is exciting. Sanctification is the process of changing. God takes me just as I am, but he will not leave me that way—I'm in for a complete overhaul, habitual conversion, learning how to fly.

The two processes must live in constant fellowship with each other—continuous justification and continuous sanctification. We can no longer keep trying to cram God into a junior-high camp experience. We need more single-eyed Christians who will habitually, tenaciously seek first the Kingdom of God. "It is all too plain that it was refusal to trust God that prevented those men from entering his rest. Now since the same promise of rest is offered to us today, let us . . . attain it . . . a full and complete rest for the people of God" (Heb. 3:19, 4:1, 10).

PREPARE FOR THE PROMISE

Although boredom and lack of meaning can be seen as the root of the leisure problem, there is also the problem of poor planning.

In his letter to the Ephesians, Paul's words about this are strong: "Live life, then, with a due sense of responsibility, not as men who do not know the meaning and purpose of life, but as those who do. Make the best use of your time, despite all the difficulties of these days. Don't be vague, but firmly grasp what you know to be the will of the Lord" (Eph. 5:15-17).

Maximum use of discretionary time demands creativity, planning, and good decision making. There is no such thing as lack of time. There is more than enough time to do what you want to if you realize that you are the master of your time, not its slave. Control starts with planning. Two keys are: (1) knowing what you want to do, and (2) planning how you are going to do it.

Have you ever stopped to make a list of your goals and priorities for your leisure time? Boredom is one of the major causes of suicide and drug abuse in our country, and yet, what folly, to dread the thought of throwing away life at once, and yet have no regard to throwing it away "by parcels and piecemeal."

PUT OFF PROCRASTINATION

The habit of always putting off an experience until you can afford it, or until the time is right, or until you know how to do it is one of the greatest burglars of joy. Be deliberate, but once you've made up your mind—jump in.

LEAVE YOUR RUTS

A sign on the Alaska Highway reads, "Choose your rut carefully. You'll be in it for the next two hundred miles." I believe in routine, but not in ruts. Routine is a form of economy; ruts are a form of fear. Dare to move out of some of the attitudes that enslave you. Take a chance. As the Irish poet, Donovan Leitch, writes:

Do what you've never done before,
See what you've never seen,
Feel what you've never felt before,
Say what you've never said,
Bear what you've never borne before,

ENOUGH IS MORE THAN ENOUGH

Hear what you've never heard.
All is not what it would seem;
Nothing ever remains the same.
Change is life's characteristic;
Bend and flow and play the game. . . .
So many times I was the one
Who stopped myself from doing things;
So many times I was the one
Who grounded myself and clipped my wings.
So I say do what you've never done before. . . .
You must go where you have never been. . . .

One of the biggest ruts for many is television—holding millions of people in our country prisoner each year. It has put more chains on more life-styles than we could ever imagine. Few have enough willpower to turn it off. Fewer have the courage not to own one. And fewer still have such an overwhelming desire to live that they would give their set away.

DEVELOP AN IDEA BOARD

Sometimes we are simply not aware of all the incredible resources available to us. I would wager, for example, that there are at least twice as many opportunities in your immediate area as you know of. It requires both some exploration and a system for keeping track of the things you find to do.

One possibility is to create a file, notebook, or bulletin board that stimulates both interest and order. Give your board a clever name and make it a priority in your family. Cut out games, ideas, notes, jokes, ads from the newspaper and other sources as a reminder of some of the possibilities. Put a special "Celebration Calendar" in the center, which notes the when and where of your next event.

MAKE LAUGHTER A PRIORITY

"He who laughs, lasts."

One of the most limiting factors to quality leisure is simply that laughter has never been high enough on the priority list. The writer of the Book of Wisdom prepared us for the New Testament reminder that joy is a fruit of the Spirit:

"A cheerful heart is a good medicine, but a downcast spirit dries up the bones" (Prov. 17:22). You can choose to be jubilant. Likewise you can choose to be gloomy. But hearty, sincere laughter is a powerful tonic for weary, battered souls.

SCHEDULE FAMILY TIME

Often we cram our schedules with our work-oriented commitments and hold tight to them, but don't do the same with the other half of our lives. Leisure is just as important.

Look at your calendar. Are you inadvertently prejudiced? Aren't your kids important enough to be on your schedule? What about your wife? Do you think it's wise to "assume" that all the special things you want to take place in their lives will just happen without planning?

My family feels differently about themselves when they see their name on my calendar ("lunch with Zac" or "dinner with Pam"). Also, my wife and I have found it critically important to schedule time together; otherwise it always seems to get erased. We try to get away for dinner at least once a week.

Likewise, we've found a need to create a family day, and then let our friends know that those days are special times. They are reserved for one of the most important priorities in my life—and I try to make sure that other commitments don't preempt it.

Along the same line, however, don't overschedule. Joy can't be overcrowded. It needs some space.

GO FOR IT!

Did you ever have to build a fire in a rainstorm realizing that you were down to your last two matches? Can you remember what it feels like to wake up at dawn with ice all over your sleeping bag? When was the last time you had half a biscuit and a finger-full of honey for dinner with a cup of tea made from a tea bag that six other people had used because there was a miscalculation in the amount of food? Have you ever been asleep only to have the Mississippi River (or so you thought) come rolling down into your sleeping bag, so you decided to stay up all night sitting around the fire in the pouring rain, laughing at the stupid jokes that somehow seem to be funnier at 4 A.M.? Have you ever slept on top of a ridge without a sleeping bag—just to see if you could do it—and awakened in the morning feeling a little taller just because you had?

Do you know what it feels like to step backward off a 100-foot cliff with some gizmo they call a six-carbiner-brake-bar tied around you, struggling to find content for words like *trust,* which were only words before? Or what it feels like to fall from a rock face and have your belayer catch you for the first time?

Have you ever walked all night under a full moon because you didn't reach your destination by sunset, and then found yourself singing in spite of your weariness because you were with some friends who felt like you did? Have you ever caught fish with your bare hands? Or started a fire with no matches? Or sat in a homemade sauna in the middle of the wilderness? Or shared your life with someone who really cared? When was the last time someone stayed up to 3 A.M. to share your laughter or your tears? Can you recall the last time you felt unique, fully alive, and like you were reaching for all your potential with all you had within you?

Have you ever wondered what the boundaries are for your physical, mental, or spiritual potential? Have you stopped recently to question what life is for? Have you asked yourself what your life is for?

Historically God's people have been uninhibited risk takers, unafraid to dive right into the heart of life. Let the herd graze where it pleases. There's more to life than riding the glass elevators at the Fairmont. Put a little pepper on your Kentucky Fried Seagull and take a chance.

What about learning how to sail, or learning how to draw, or directing a play? What about learning to scuba dive, or taking a vacation on as little money as possible? Adventure has a lot of different names, all of which add flavor to life.

The irony is that memorable leisure—the kind that has gravity and substance—often requires an inventive kind of boldness that is eager to take on new experiences, a desire to be a participant rather than a spectator. A certain amount of aggressiveness is necessary to seek out all the possibilities and explore them. A person has to be willing to fail, to try something totally foreign.

But there is an unmatchable dignity in experiences like these. The spirit seems to rise to the occasion and fills the places in your life that you didn't even know existed before. You stand a little taller, your feet a little firmer. There is an assurance that flows from these kinds of encounters that no longer has a need to compare, demand, accuse, justify, or excuse. There is a sense of inner calm and inner directedness that seems to occur naturally as a result—and all of life takes on a new perspective. This is leisure at its best. These are peak experiences that become reference points during the inevitable droughts. They become memories that do more than just hang on the wall. Experiences like these redefine the limits of our capabilities, our personalities, and provide living seminars for personal wholeness. We become aware of the world around us again—tasting the salt air, feeling the thirst of the desert, hearing the wind blow, being encompassed by the overwhelming fragrance that a field of flowers can provide.

Recently many have awakened to these kinds of possibilities and through it have not only redefined leisure, but life itself. It's time we let go of some of our insipid images of leisure to include those experiences that push us to the limits. Experiences like these have changed the lives of countless people. One of my greatest privileges has been to work with the people of Summit Expedition. Through these adventures, I've seen people come alive to themselves and to God in ways I would have never dreamed possible.

Why not you? Before you exclude yourself from such activities, make sure you know the facts. Summit Expedition, and programs like it, have had people from ages fourteen to seventy on their courses. Just this week I read of a seventy-year-old woman in northern California who just *started* running marathons. And she's eagerly looking forward to the adventure that lies ahead of her. How often we limit ourselves before we even start. Too few of us realize that our leisure time can become, if we allow it, a source of wholeness and excellence for us.

Recently a young man named Bruce Jennings from Newport Beach, California, cycled from the west coast of the United States to the east coast. What made it unusual was that he had only one leg.

Pete Strudwick will be running marathons again this year in some of his spare time. What is admirable is that Pete was born without hands or feet. Many of us are more handicapped by our attitudes than by any physical inconvenience.

A Spanish translation of John 1:1 says, "En el principeo era el Verbo, y el Verbo era con Dios, y el Verbo era Dios," which translated literally means "In the beginning was the Verb, and the Verb was with God, and the Verb was God." I don't know of any logical reason why God should cease to be a verb in our lives just because we have reached a particular age, or we have bodily limitations.

What hinders you right now from becoming the man or woman of God whom you would like to be? The typical view of the Christian life is one of deliverance *from* trouble. Scripture, however, calls us to deliverance *in* trouble. The difference is not just a semantic one. Human beings are much like bicycles or cars—they are much easier to steer if they are moving. It's crucial that we keep the flow of God's Spirit active, and refuse to give in to circumstance or discouragement. In the introduction to his book on survival skills, Larry Dean Olsen shares an appropriate anecdote about a man lost in the desert, and what an important role our attitude plays in our survival:

"He has been out of food and water for days. His lips

are swollen, his tongue is swollen, he's all beat up and bloody. Some of his bones are almost peeking through. He has been just scraped and beat up by the cactus and sand and sun. He's blistered. As he is crawling over this little hill he comes across this little plant and he props himself up on one bloody elbow and looks down at this plant and he says, 'You know, if things keep going like this I might get discouraged!' "[4]

God wants to penetrate our attitudes so he can free us up to stick our noses right into the heart of life wherever we are.

Mere survival of these times is not sufficient. One of the problems inherent in man's tremendous abilities is his ability to adapt to almost anything. The danger is that we begin to simply endure our seasons rather than celebrate them, and we let life slip away imperceptibly by the mere passage of time.

It is time to come out of hibernation and improve the quality of our lives by giving a resounding Yes to the Now, by giving ourselves permission to reexperience newer, deeper, more profound levels of life.

11
LET LIFE HAPPEN

Life and Time are our only real possessions.

Unknown

To me, every hour of light and dark is a miracle, every inch of space is a miracle.

Walt Whitman
Miracles

BALANCE IS A DELICATE ART. Now that I have (hopefully) convinced you of the importance of effort, of seizing each day, of the rigorous discipline necessary for quality leisure, let me present the other side, which is just as true. We have spoken of deliberately living according to priorities, of bursting out of ruts, of purposely moving into cul-de-sacs of impossibility in order to discover more of ourselves, of life, and of God.

But all the discipline in the world cannot make the sun rise any earlier, or a flower more fragrant, or a smile more spontaneous. Running five miles a day will add as much as a hundred miles of capillaries to your system, make you feel more alive, and allow you to go places and do things you've never done before, but it won't necessarily teach you how to laugh. You don't have to have a plan to clap your hands. As someone once said, "If you have to move even ten inches from where you are now in order to be happy, then you will never be truly happy."

Working harder at your leisure does not automatically mean that you enjoy it more. It only widens the perspective and deepens the capacity. But you can't bulldoze your way into pleasure. Effort can plow the ground and remove the weeds, but it can't make it a garden of gratitude.

There are two kinds of assets to quality leisure— graceful discipline, and disciplined grace. The first deals with big commitments, the latter with the life of little commitments. The first pushes the light to the limits, the second bathes in the generosity of the light given. The former climbs higher, the latter sees the beauty along the way.

One of the finest teachers I had in college had a singular purpose for his art class. He said, "I want you to learn how to use your eyes for something more than just to keep from bumping into things." Graceful discipline is what will get you up at sunrise, but disciplined grace is what opens your eyes to see it. Graceful discipline is primarily interested in seeking, the other in finding. One wants to spend its vacation hiking across the Grand Canyon; the other wants to absorb every inch of joy and beauty along the way. When someone is striving and seeking, sometimes it happens quite easily that he sees only the thing he is seeking. He is unable to find anything else or absorb anything else because he is focused exclusively on the thing he is seeking. So conscious of the goal, he misses the miracles along the way. How often this happens to successful businessmen, who aim for an illusory goal called success, and don't see that the life they were seeking was right under their noses all along.

Graceful discipline *makes* life happen. It is aggressive, courageous, scheduled, disciplined. Disciplined grace *lets* life happen. It is receptive, but not passive; deliberate, but not necessarily unchangeable; spontaneous, but not living at loose ends. Both require discipline. And both are very necessary. Together they not only complement each other, but they synergize each other. *Synergy* was a term central to the vocabulary of Buckminster Fuller, indicating that the total effect is greater than the sum of their effects when acting independently. As he would express it, one plus one can sometimes equal four, which is the spiritual principle basic to Body Life.

Enough is enough—if not more than enough. If I can be satisfied with little, then enough becomes a banquet. Peace is both a process of panting after God's own heart, and also letting him find you. Because you are found, you are free to seek. And you find that the God at the end of the journey is the same one you knew at the beginning. Learning to let life happen rediscovers the importance of small things. It relishes childlike joys of the everyday wonders of being alive. "Yet they seek me daily and delight to know my ways" (Isa. 58: 2).

Some of God's miracles are small. Some of God's truths are quite simple. If you cannot do great things for God, do small things in a great way. Small things can be not only beautiful but life-giving. Yield to them.

Have you forgotten how to enjoy the fragrance of the flowers in your front yard? When was the last time you were touched by wonder? Can you find joy in a paper cup of time or a thimbleful of love? Or are you one of those sadly described by the Psalmist, who "have ears, but do not hear; noses, but do not smell. They have hands, but do not feel; feet, but do not walk" (Ps. 115: 6-7).

Many of us still have tragically limited understandings of grace. Unknowingly we still serve a God we think is stingy, who loves us only in proportion to how much we work for him, who is embarrassed by laughter and surprised by spontaneity. We have forgotten, or never realized, that each day is a gift—we did nothing to deserve it. We've forgotten, or refused out of arrogance to believe, that each breath is a gift, and all the work in the world won't give us more. We've forgotten, or never learned, that the mark of a believer is not only love but joy, wonder, appreciation, surprise, creativity, peace, tenacity, hope, simplicity, and even play.

When was the last time you saw something you've never seen before or smelled something you've never smelled before—in your own backyard? It's not so much the ability to sing but the desire to sing that counts. As Joan Anglund says, "A bird doesn't sing because he has an answer; he sings because he has a song."[1]

Can you imagine the tragedy of having all that you desire right at your fingertips and not appreciating it? Can you imagine the sadness of seeing someone squinting at the horizon desperately, while what he is looking for is right at his feet? Can you imagine the despair of searching the world over for God's goodness, and not seeing it in your own family?

Prayer is both a discipline and a process of grace. Play is likewise. Both are, in a sense, useless—but I cannot imagine living without either.

May God open us to the little things in life—so that our hearts don't grow old. May he teach us to be supple and thirsty for the everyday wonders of being alive—so that our minds won't grow weary. May he help us not to have to be so useful that we become useless.

Children are again probably our best teachers in this regard, for they seem to know how to let life hug them.

ENOUGH IS MORE THAN ENOUGH

One of their philosopher friends, Winnie-the-Pooh, expressed disciplined grace well: "poetry and hums aren't things which you get, they are things which get you. And all you can do is go where they find you."[2]

Probably the best example in our house occurred one evening at the dinner table. Zachary was so overtaken by the day that he was singing a little homemade song:

"I was walking along and saw a dog—and he said bow wow. And the cat said meow, and the cow said moo. And as I was walking along I saw some flowers. . . ."

There was a rather long pause, so I asked innocently, "And what did they say?"

"And they said, 'Jesus loves me, this I know, for the Bible tells me so.' "

When I was four, God was everywhere. I hope, as I grow older and wiser, that I will learn that again. My sons will help me—if I will but listen. The flowers will teach me—if only I have ears like his to hear.

12
HOW TO
TAKE A VACATION

If happiness could be found in having material things, and in being able to indulge yourself in things that you consider pleasurable, then we, in America, would be deliriously happy. We would be telling one another frequently of our unparalleled bliss, rather than trading tranquilizer prescriptions.

John Gardner
Self-Renewal

ANY IDEA THAT IS NOT A LITTLE DANGEROUS is probably not worth being called an idea. As A. N. Whitehead said, "It's the business of the future to be dangerous." This is the dangerous part of this book. For the last many pages, we have talked about the misconceptions of leisure, the real meaning and purpose of leisure, and the principles of quality leisure. Now it is time to test some of these ideas in a more practical manner.

Many get to this point and want to move, but hesitate because of lack of specific direction. The real test of this book is not just whether or not you like it, but whether you are willing to do something about it. The acid test occurs when you lay this book down.

ENOUGH IS MORE THAN ENOUGH

It seems to be getting easier and easier these days to thrive on the vicarious experience of others—through spectator sports, TV dramas, personality magazines, and yes, even books. But secondhand experience results only in dissatisfaction. The more we experience life directly, the deeper our joy. One of the greatest insults we pay God is to say we are bored.

What can we do to start living life directly? This chapter and the two that follow offer some specific suggestions. We'll start with perhaps the most familiar form of leisure—the vacation.

VACATION KILLERS

"Having a lousy time. Wish I weren't here." Why are so many vacations losers? Some people experience disappointment year after year and never know why. Here are a few thoughts that might help.

Don't overwait. Some people demand a reason for everything, and thus don't take a vacation until they desperately need one—when they are physically and emotionally exhausted, or ill. Even a trip to Paradise would be hard pressed to make up those odds.

Don't overdo. Since they've waited fifty weeks for this vacation, some people try to cram a year's worth of living into two weeks. They wind up pushing harder and spending longer hours than they do on the job. Rushing from one place to the next, "hurrying to be happy," it's no wonder that peace eludes them.

Don't overexpect. Related to this image that vacation is a reward for hard work is the notion that therefore we are *supposed* to enjoy this time, and if we don't, we feel anxious. We carry so many bionic images of leisure into the vacation that nothing could ever match it—and then wonder why we're so unhappy.

To anticipate that a place can make you happy because a full-page ad says it can is inviting a letdown. Likewise to be impatient because your last purchase didn't make you ecstatic is sheer nonsense. Yet each day, more of us slide into this subtle trap, mainly because we don't want to be responsible for our own enjoyment. We want to pay someone else to make us happy. But it doesn't work that way. Joy must spring from within.

How do we begin to bring more life into our leisure, and particularly our vacations? One of the biggest steps is recognizing that we might have some difficulties with leisure time. A large part of the solution to any problem lies in an honest recognition that it exists. This awareness may lead to a change in behavior, and that prospect may be a little frightening. But the risk is worth taking. What specific steps might help if you are the victim of vacation blues?

VACATION CHECKLIST

1. Have reasonable expectations rather than impossible ones, ones that invariably lead to disappointment. A vacation will not necessarily make you a new person or salvage a troubled marriage. But it can, and will, be refreshing—if you let it be.

2. Examine some of your past vacations. Be objective, but be compassionate. Don't vilify yourself, no matter how your past trips have turned out. Just try to think of ways they could be improved.

3. Relax. Don't hurry past the beauty. Joy is a gentle and delicate living thing. Let it happen.

4. Don't take yourself too seriously. Expect some obstacles. Embrace them. Even laugh at them if you can. Convert them into part of your vacation. Make an adventure out of your inevitable mishaps. Murphy's Law—which says that if anything can possibly go wrong, it will not only do so, but at the worst possible time—still has a habit of inviting itself on a lot of vacations. Don't let it ruin yours.

5. Be creative. Put a little variety into your celebrations. Don't let someone from a travel agency plan your happiness. Let your imaginative juices flow. Make each vacation a once-in-a-lifetime experience.

6. Take *all* of you on vacation. Use all of your senses. This is a time when you can be whole, when you can use your smeller for something more than just to hang your glasses on, and those funny-looking contraptions on the side of your head for something more than just to keep your hat off your shoulders. Don't just eat; taste your food. Let your vacation be a five-sense event.

7. Plan a strategy for vacation diet. Enjoy your food, but don't make it the whole purpose of your vacation. Resistance is usually a little lower during vacations. Fatigue, frustration, or even boredom sometimes stimulate indulgence. Have a plan.

" 'By golly,' shouted Lizzie's husband, as he pushed the third brioche of the continental breakfast under her nose while vacationing in Paris, 'we're paying for it, we're gonna eat it.' Normally Lizzie's breakfast at home amounted to 200 calories. Her vacation breakfast that day: 1,000 calories."[1]

Without some forethought, overeating can ruin a vacation. Take low-calorie snacks for those long rides in the car, and remember that the famous response to why something was done—"because it's there"—was meant for climbing mountains, not eating.

8. Get regular exercise. Not only will this help you control your diet, but it will also help you enjoy your trip. A good balance between rest and activity is best.

9. Take short vacations if long ones make you homesick, especially if you are taking one of those special getaways without the kids. But make sure you give yourself enough time to unwind fully.

10. Forget such maxims as "Hard work deserves a rest." Don't spend all your time justifying your vacation. A vacation isn't just a dessert for a job well done. Enjoy it for what it is—time to live.

11. Break your routine. Get up at a different time than you usually do during the year. If you never get to read—read. If you read as part of your job—put down the books for a few weeks. Let some new light into your life.

12. Do something unusual. Be an experimenter. Meet new people, try new experiences. Let people think you're loony. Wear a funny hat or put your shirt on backwards for a day. Roller-skate down a shopping mall. Climb a mountain, or a tree. Don't wear a watch for a week. Hug a tree, fly a kite, wear a button, jog in triangles. Fool somebody. Fool two somebodies. Go for a long walk in your barefeet. Poke some holes in your rigidity. This is not a time to be timid. Take a chance. It's worth it.

13. Do something a little extravagant. Buy something you've always wanted. Let go a little bit. Don't be so reasonable all the time.

14. Learn something new on your vacation. One of the great joys in life is learning. Teach yourself to play chess, or learn to needlepoint. Learn calligraphy and send fancy postcards to all your friends. Uncover some of those talents you've been hiding.

15. Learn to look for the best and laugh at the worst. You will usually see what you are looking for. Choose to

see the good, the best, the beautiful. Also choose to laugh at the crazy things that always want to go on vacation with you—flat tires, flat hair, flat spirits, flat experiences. A couple summers ago when melting ice caused a river to flood our campsite, a friend woke me with the comment that "the dew was a little heavier this morning." No one can make you depressed but yourself.

16. Give yourself permission to be happy. Practice it. Work hard to eliminate that free-floating guilt that still says you should be working or doing something more useful, and that you shouldn't be having such a good time. Let your restless spirit relax for a few moments. Let your cup overflow. Fruit is simply the excess of life. You can't try to bear fruit; you've got to let it happen.

17. Let the hero out in you. Live each day and each vacation as if it were your last opportunity. Rejoice and crack the skies with laughter. Let your passion for being alive and being one of God's people encourage you to be the very best you can be. Put forth the best qualities of your personality to each person and each situation you meet—and in giving it away, much of it will contagiously rub off on you.

13
IDEAS
FOR
ACTIVE REST

"Why did Mister God rest on the seventh day?" she began.
"I suppose he was a bit flaked out after six days hard work," I
answered.
"He didn't rest cause he was tired, though."
"Oh, didn't he? It makes me tired just to think about it all."
"Course he didn't. He wasn't tired."
"Wasn't he?"
"No, he made *rest."*

Fynn
Mister God, This Is Anna

VACATIONS DON'T HAVE TO BE ESCAPES—they can be
introductions. They shouldn't always be vacations *from*
something (a vacation from the kids, from the routine,
etc.). Perhaps what you need is a vacation *to*. This chapter
will describe some unusual ideas for vacations both *to* and
from.

Vacation designs need to vary according to your purpose. Before you start planning your next vacation, you

115

should know (1) what your particular needs are at this time in your life (rest? activity? change of scenery? solitude?) and (2) what your hopes are. Then these factors should be woven together as you create your living vacation.

VACATIONS *TO*

A vacation *to* is a purposeful exploration of varying length (from a few hours to a few weeks) of a specific idea that appeals to you. Some of the things you must remember are to travel light, don't spend all your time driving, have a specific purpose in mind (even if it's being "nonpurposeful" for a few hours), be a little daring, and enjoy it with all your senses. Here are a few ideas to get you going:

1. *Health vacations.* If you're feeling a little sluggish, maybe you need to spend some time focusing on yourself and your health. As Anna said, "And we're out to love God with all our hearts, to love our friends, and don't forget to take some time to love ourselves."[1] Love yourself by taking some days to develop some solid health patterns. It may be a tennis vacation, a jogging vacation on the coast, a cycling vacation to some friends, or a hiking vacation in the mountains. Work on filling your lungs with a lot of oxygen, your mind with a lot of good thoughts, and your body with a lot of good food.

2. *Educational vacations.* Have you ever thought of taking some vacation time with the specific intent of learning something new? You may want to learn how to fix a car, or do woodwork, or rock-climb. You may go somewhere to learn how to paint or cook, or set aside special time at

home to take classes at a local college.

3. *Back-roads vacations.* Some friends recently spent their entire vacation on back roads. What stories they had to tell about friendly people they met and unusual places they saw. Part of the adventure was in planning how to get there using only back roads; the other part was enjoying all the serendipitous events that naturally happen on such a trip.

4. *Children's vacations.* Let your children plan and, as much as possible, implement a short vacation. It might be very exciting seeing the world from their eyes. Stay flexible, and plan on a lot of surprises.

5. *Cheap vacations.* These can be some of the most inventive kind ever. The purpose here is to discover how *much* you can do with as little money as possible (many of you have had a lot of practice already). For example, how many things can you do for twenty-five cents? How about one dollar? What can your whole family do for five dollars? Look in the newspapers for all the free films and exhibits you can go to. List all the places you can explore for nothing. There are more than you might normally think. Keep a scrapbook of ideas, or put them on your bulletin board in bright and funny colors. How far can you travel on seventy-nine cents? How creative are you at eating for a day on $1.12? The ideas are endless—and the results in joy and how you feel about yourself are worth more than the money you save.

6. *Sunset Magazine vacations.* Many of us want our houses to look like *Better Homes and Gardens* instead of *Popular Mechanics,* but we need time to develop ideas that will fit our particular Quonset hut. Why not take the time? Set aside time with the fixed aim of getting ideas (and having fun). Leave the children home this time and go see different kinds of architecture, color patterns, fences, and porch designs. Then take a sketch pad and

talk of all the wild possibilities over dinner. If you have a lot of good ideas, go to a motel for an evening and continue the conversation.

7. *Reinventory vacations.* Has it ever occured to you to take time to remember what is special to you? We can get so busy that we forget what's really important. What about taking an overnight vacation, or maybe a weekend, and resolve to redefine your values (and try to figure out how to implement them)?

Start with your lifetime goal. Do you know what it is? Do you know it with enough clarity to write it down? What are some of your lifetime dreams? Your priorities? Are you living in accordance with them these days? How could you improve? It's important to be specific.

Take whatever resources along with you that you might need (Bible, writing material, tapes, other books, etc.), but don't forget that unhurried and uncrowded time will be your most important resource.

8. *Memory lane vacations.* Revisit some of those special places that have been hallmarks in your life. Take the time to see old friends. Spend some evenings remembering, laughing, telling stories, and maybe even going through some of the old annuals. Relish the nostalgia for a while.

9. *Evangelistic vacations.* Bill and Carolyn Young recently took a delightful vacation to Oregon, where their distinct purpose was to share their faith in Jesus Christ. In doing so they revitalized not only the lives of a lot of other people but their own as well. Their relationship grew stronger because they really needed each other, and their faith grew because of the challenge.

10. *Just Being vacations.* Take off your watch for a while. Forget what time it is. Eat when you're hungry instead of at noon. Reestablish your relationship with God, with your lifetime companion, and with yourself on

the basis of who you are rather than what you do.

Pam and I were sharing a weekend like this in the mountains last year at a friend's cabin when I looked over and noticed that the alarm clock had no hands. It was nice to think that nothing could alarm us, and that we had discovered, at least for a while, some untime. Untime like this can be dictated by spontaneity. Travel very light, plan very little, lead with your heart, and let life surprise you around every corner. Leave spacious "do nothing time" for doing what you feel like. Take long "nothing walks" for the sole purpose of enjoying the walk. Get in touch with your feet and your body again. Read fairy tales and poetry, take naps, and realize that you are, and that that is enough.

11. *Vacations you train for.* This summer my wife and I are planning to ride our bikes in southern Oregon for a specified distance. Part of the joy has been in the training necessary—we're training for a purpose. Select a purpose and make a vacation out of getting ready for it.

12. *Seeing vacations.* Have you ever thought of deliberately spending some days (either at home or traveling) to discover the magic of seeing? We take our eyes for granted so often and use them just to keep from bumping into things. Said Helen Keller, "I have walked with people whose eyes are full of light but who see nothing in sea or sky, nothing in city streets, nothing in books. It were far better to sail forever in the night of blindness . . . than to be content with the mere act of looking without seeing."[2]

See color, for example. Follow one color for the whole day. You will be amazed at how much you've been blind to. Sit quietly on the grass and allow your eyes to marvel at the world around you. A bush, a cloud, or a leaf might become an unforgettable experience. Draw a circle about six feet in diameter around you and see as many things as you can within that "magic circle." Your eyes will never be the same.

We do a lot of looking everyday: through lenses, telescopes, television tubes. We look more and more, but see less and less. Unless we slow down to see more than just labels and directions, we become merely spectators, and in the Kingdom of God no one can see as long as he remains just a spectator.

Seeing vacations can be expanded upon. Take along a camera, and photograph the splendor you see. If you like, choose to focus on seeing and photographing faces for a day. Another possibility is to take a pencil and sketch pad, and explore your artistic talents. Drawing, says Frederick Franck, is the discipline by which he constantly rediscovers the world. You can't beat that for a vacation.

13. *A wonder trip.* As you did with seeing, now explore the magnificence of life with all your senses. Unwrap some of the incredible gifts of life around you. There is so much more there than normally meets the eye. Take time to ask questions rather than seek answers. How does grass grow up through cement? How does a bird fly? How do grunion know to ride the high tide? There are thousands of questions, which, like treasure chests, are waiting for your exploration. As Thomas Carlyle said, "The man who cannot wonder is but a pair of spectacles behind which there is no eyes."[3]

14. *Gourmet vacations.* Rediscover that food is something more than stuffing. Turn an evening into a mini vacation by immersing yourself without inhibition into the life of a gourmet. Dress in your fanciest. Eat very slowly, tasting every morsel. Feast on the candlelight atmosphere as well. Ask the waiter complex questions on how the food was prepared—and then take a menu home for memories.

15. *Change of life-style or service vacations.* Not all leisure

has to be leisure to be enjoyable. What about taking your family to the midwest to work on a farm, or to help friends build a house? What about arranging a long trip with a truckdriver you know? Or volunteering your services at a hospital or a convalescent home? Albert Schweitzer said late in his life, "The only ones among you who will be truly happy are those who have sought and found how to serve."

16. *Exploration vacations.* Your only limit here is creativity. Explore a friendship through traveling together on a vacation. Explore a book or an idea. Jack Meyer, a very special friend of mine, has devoted this year to studying the thought of C. S. Lewis. He is pursuing—through reading, travel, discussion with friends, media, and any other source of information—to know and understand this great Christian thinker.

17. *Once-in-a-lifetime specials.* There are so many things to do that we will probably do only once. Design a day around going for a ride in a helicopter, or going to a horse race. Find a bookbinder and find out how books are bound. Take a weekend to go skydiving or shoot the rapids. Do something a little eccentric, like going to an umbrella factory or following the whole process behind the making of toilet paper. It might be great fun—and will probably be a terrific conversation stopper at your next party.

18. *One parent, one child occasions.* Make a midget vacation out of spending quality time alone with one of your children. It can just be dinner together, or it can be a whole weekend trip. You might participate in an event together or explore an idea together. (If she's younger, you might have a little vacation "learning to be a lady.") A father-son rock climbing venture, where each has to belay the other on the end of a rope, might introduce lifelong qualities to the relationship. (Good ideas on this

area are available in *Dads Only,* an ingenious and very readable monthly newsletter for busy fathers; P.O. Box 20594, San Diego, CA 92120.)

19. *Rest vacations.* In an article entitled "How to Conquer the Spiritual Blahs," Bill Bright focused at one point on the spiritual problems that have their source in sheer physical fatigue. Some of us need the kind of vacation that has rest as its undeviating purpose. Go somewhere where no one can find you, take the phone off the hook, and spend most of the days horizontal. Give yourself permission to get recharged. Give your body a breather. It could be the vacation that will get you prepared for the rest of your vacations.

20. *The third honeymoon.* Have you taken time to experience your second honeymoon yet? If not, you'll have to do that first. The purpose of honeymoon specials is to take time to remember who you are married to, and why. If you have a copy of your wedding vows, bring them along and reread them. If not, maybe you'll want to start your little rehoneymoon after attending the wedding of some friends. Maybe you will take time to write new vows that pertain especially to your commitment to each other during the second season of your marriage.

Other ideas include such things as going back to the place where you had your original honeymoon, making something special for each other with your hands, framing some of the special photos from your marriage and honeymoon, reading a book out loud together, having something special engraved for the one you love, spending an afternoon or evening together, writing a journal of all the special events in your marriage, writing a poem together, and writing down ten things you'd like to do together in the next year.

As you can see, ideas for bringing more variety and

fulfillment into your life through vacationing are plentiful. Obviously, there are many, many more. Maybe one of your family mini vacations could be a brainstorming session to list the ones not touched upon here—such as historical vacations, underwater vacations, a "Roots" vacation, primitive vacations, and the like.

VACATIONS *FROM*

Not only are there vacations that have a distinct purpose of going *to* something, but there can likewise be a rainbow of possibilities of important vacations *from* something. Consider, if you will, some of the following twenty-four-hour vacations from aspects of life that might limit you in some way:

1. *Vacation from words.* A twenty-four-hour mini vacation from words might not only be very peaceful, but might also bring new insight into their value. We speak, as I understand it, more than five thousand words in a day. A quiet revolution might occur if we didn't have them for a day.

2. *Vacation from food.* It's commonly called a fast, rather than a vacation—but who says you can't change your attitude to make it a celebration rather than an endurance contest. It's one of the most important little vacations I know. If done with regularity, it will change not only your weight but also your life-style.

3. *A vacation from seeing or hearing.* Some years ago I taped my eyes for a good part of a week so that I was totally blind. That time probably taught me more about my senses than any five books could have done. It was the first time I realized that my nose could do more than get

broken. I did it with a friend who served as my guide. Dick was an aggressive learner and teacher, so he had me do things like go running with him, jump off a fifteen-foot tower into a lake, write a letter, and find my way out of the woods alone—so my experience was enhanced greatly. Since then I've intentionally limited other senses in order to isolate and experience them. They have all been priceless life investments.

4. *Vacation from complaining.* One of the assignments I frequently give my students is to try to go twenty-four hours without complaining. It is undoubtedly one of the toughest assignments they have during the entire year. No one has successfully made it yet—but the experience of trying it is poignant, painful, and enlightening. Few of us are aware of the extent of our complaining. Attempting such a "vacation" will bring you to your knees in humility. Have some friends do it, too, the same day. Take notes during the day of your experiences, and then get together a few days later to discuss it. It may bring about some important changes.

Not all of these mini vacations have to be limited to twenty-four hours. You may want, for example, to take a one-week to six-month vacation from your television just to learn more about its influence in your life. You may choose to design a vacation from your telephone for a period of time. Some have decided to take a vacation from meat or sugar. The joy and the challenge is again twofold—first, to diagnose those things that you may feel to be keeping you from your best, and second, to design a creative and pleasant mini vacation.

14

IDEAS FOR
MAXI AND MINI
VACATIONS

If I am content with little, enough is as good as a feast.
Isaac Bickerstaff

HAVE YOU EVER THOUGHT OF TAKING a two-minute vacation? "Too short," you say? Guess again.

What about a three-year vacation? Too long? Too impractical? It all depends on how you view the word *vacation.*

Who ever said all vacations had to be two weeks long? Breathe some fresh air into your thinking. As varied as the types of vacations are their potential lengths.

If you are "vacating" only once a year (the usual thought pattern), that two-week block of time almost suffocates in the desperate attempt to do a whole year's worth of living in that time. Putting all your vacational eggs in one basket is ineffective and usually leads to depression. We would do much better to plan more consistent and more frequent breaks, each with a different purpose, to meet the various needs of our family.

ENOUGH IS MORE THAN ENOUGH
SUPER-MAXI VACATIONS

A super-maxi vacation experience is the fruit of a lot of planning, togetherness, and courage. It's not really a vacation—it is a family experience that combines all their vacation thoughts for the year. No one I know of can afford six months to a year off, but most families could draw together what might be called "a string of pearls." This is an extended, full-bodied, sometimes challenging, sometimes relaxing warehouse of opportunities bound together not only by the participants but also by a theme of what you've chosen to do. It might be, for example, that you decide the year will be the "Year of Adventure." You might do such things as learn how to sail, rock-climb, skydive, and do karate during the course of that year. Or you could take on an adventure of the mind or spirit like learning how to meditate on Bible passages. Other possibilities include taking a year to simplify your life-style, or devoting a year to developing spartan health habits, or learning to build grandfather clocks.

MAXI VACATIONS

Some people have jobs that give them extended periods off. Usually these individuals are rather creative in their use of this time, but a few ideas never hurt. The main suggestion is to do something for someone else. Put all that you would normally do one year into helping build a camp or creating a recreational area for an orphanage. Focus on specific persons or projects. Seeing your efforts change lives will bring considerably more joy than spending five hundred dollars to go somewhere fancy and learn how to lie in the sun.

A war correspondent tells a story of coming across a nun on her knees patiently swabbing the gangrenous leg of a very sick young soldier lying on a mat. Revulsed by the scene, he had to turn his head away. Finally he said to her, "Sister, I wouldn't do that for a million dollars."

The nun paused momentarily, and said, "Neither would I."

Some uses of our so-called free time transcend anything that money could buy.

Most people have pretty good handles on what might be considered normal-sized vacations, but are at a loss as to what to do with the little lumps of time. Hence, I'll skip over the family-size and the regular-size range and jump into mini, midget, and two-minute vacations.

MINI VACATIONS

Most of us fail to realize that we have built into our calendars fifty-two miniature vacations every year. With a little planning and creativity, these can be meaningful and joyful times.

The principle of one day out of every seven for worship and rest has been true since creation, but I know of very few people who take that commandment seriously. I still struggle with it. Again and again William McNamara's comments about learning how to "waste" that time for God's sake come back to haunt me. "There is only one way to truly celebrate the Sabbath—and that is to waste it prodigiously. Until I can waste time prodigiously I do not take God seriously. If Christ is real, he must be able to hold me and captivate me."[1] It is my acknowledgment of his sovereignty.

There must be a reason why rest was included in Creation, in the Ten Commandments, and why Jesus said that the Sabbath was made for man. There must be a reason why the Sabbath is fifty-two times more important than any other "holy-day."

We need to break the habit of looking in the TV guide for our happiness each weekend. Plan some small trips where you drive less than two hours. Adopt the following three principles:

- Stay together
- Learn the flowers
- Travel lightly

Take as few "props" as possible. Also leave behind such excess baggage as worry, guilt, anxiety, and depression. Up your surprisability factor a couple notches and take off. My wife and I call it "Fresno-ing," because for a while our only vacations were mini ones, where we went into Fresno, got a motel—and just had the time of our lives doing simple things like going for a swim, going to a bookstore, taking in a movie, and having a quiet dinner together.

What about limiting your mini vacation to one tank of gas—going anywhere you can and investing yourself as much as you can? What about a "one meal" vacation, meaning that you do what you can in your local area over a time period limited to one meal (you can go from right after breakfast until a late dinner, or longer if you discipline those hunger pangs). What about celebrating a Sunday by simply being alive to the leading of the Holy Spirit for a whole day? Itineraries are not allowed.

Have you ever had a "ludicrous Thursday lunch"? They were invented by a madcap genius friend of mine named Ray Rood. They can happen any day of the week, or even any time during the day, for that matter. Their singular purpose is to celebrate life with a little madness. Either spontaneous phone calls are made or formal invitations are sent out, designating a time and place. Meals are usually only a fabricated excuse to laugh at the funny things in life, especially in your own life. The atmosphere works almost like a magnet, drawing out the sad and difficult things into the light, and sharing them over a meal doused with laughter. The basic precept is that "if we don't all do something crazy, we might all go insane."

What about amplifying the meaning of a holiday with a little imagination, and then jumping in without a safety belt? On Valentine's Day this year, Zac and Joshua and I got up early, dressed up like Valentine Fairies (don't ask me what a Valentine Fairy looks like), cut out about two hundred little red hearts which we proceeded to place all over the house in the form of little "trails," and then we all went in and woke up mom. While she was following these strange trails all over the house, finding a little love-note or surprise at various junctions, Zac and I fixed a splendiferous "Breakfast for a Queen."

Some may say we're a little strange—but I'm beginning to realize that it might be a compliment. I'm not sure I want to be "normal" anymore. Some may think it's not worth the effort, but it would have been hard to convince Pam of that that morning (and us too).

I'm beginning to believe that God likes misfits. Christianity does not consist in abstaining from doing things no gentleman would think of doing, says R. L. Sheppard, but in doing things that are unlikely to occur to anyone who is not in touch with the Spirit of Christ.[2]

We have the power to convert any situation into a mission of gladness. Ben and Loretta Patterson told us recently of another incident in the life of their vibrant mother, who is now in her eighties. She was standing in a rather lengthy line waiting for some tickets. The line hadn't moved and the rain wouldn't stop. Rather than just be dismal, she asked someone to save her place in line for a few moments. A short time later she returned with thirty doughnuts, which she proceeded to give away to cheer everybody up. She had converted a rather dull moment into a magic one.

"The people around us can always read our hearts by our faces. The inner things we live with will always show up on our faces. The soul is dyed with the color of our commitment. Our task is not to argue, philosophize, speculate, cajole, but to live a life that demands an explanation. Is there anything about us that would force people to say, 'Now that's living! That's the way I wish I could live!' A joy-filled life will always demand an explanation—but too often we want Life without having to change our life-style."[3]

What about anniversaries? Do you remember them? If you do, have you bogged down to the same routine of dinner and roses? Are you aware of the fact, for example, that each year has a different symbol—like the fifth year being wood, and the ninth year being pottery? Do you ever make something or find something to commemorate these events? Or are you still in too much of a hurry?

What about birthdays? Are parties really just for kids? Don't tell my wife or friends that—because this year they really surprised me. Pam rented a whole room at a restaurant and had friends come do a "Tim Hansel Roast." I don't know who had more fun, them or me.

We are surrounded with endless natural occasions for joy if we would but take advantage of them. What about making buttons this year to celebrate Columbus Day? Or be like Maureen Hoffman who even went so far as to celebrate "Garbage Day." She made special buttons to wear and share commemorating the men who work so hard to keep our cans empty. She even had buttons and signs for "One day after garbage day" and "Garbage day is only two days away." Now that's celebrating the ordinary.

MIDGET VACATIONS

Midget vacations fall along the same idea, but take even less time. We're called not only to structure sufficient time into each week for rest, recreation, and worship—but also into each day. Jim Carlson recently shared with me his idea for "a daily Sabbath." He said that if we're to tithe 10 percent of our energy and finances to the Lord, then shouldn't we do it with our time as well? Basically he said that 10 percent of each day would be 2.4 hours—and he's trying to develop the discipline that will allow him to creatively dedicate that time to knowing and enjoying God more.

Midget vacations open our eyes to all that we have right at our feet, right in our own home. It might include trying to go outside every morning for a week and see something you've never seen before. Just because you've lived in the same house for twenty years doesn't mean you've seen everything.

Here are some other "morning midgets" you might want to try.

• Praise God for the sunrise (that means you have to be up to see it). I heard someone say that one of the greatest tragedies in the world today is that people no longer see the sunrise.

• Don't get out of bed until you can think of one thing you're thankful for, and secondly, say, "This is the day that the Lord has made, let us rejoice and be glad" (and really mean it).

• Go outside and yell (as loud as your inhibitions will allow), "Life, I love you!"

• Hug something or someone.

• Instead of saying your normal grace before breakfast, either (a) sing a song, (b) whistle, (c) clap, or (d) just stomp your feet. In other words, praise him with your whole body, instead of just your lips.

• Phone somebody and wish them a happy day.

• Try to find something in your yard or house that you've never seen before. You'll be surprised at how many there are.

• Laugh at least once by the time breakfast is over.

• My father-in-law went to a seminar on goal setting, and he heard the speaker share a very unique goal: to be happy by eight o'clock. In other words, refuse to be controlled by your circumstances.

• Do something special for yourself in the morning—make yourself a special cup of tea, kiss your wife, pat your dog, read a favorite section of Scripture. In other words, help yourself set the pace for the day.

• Smile at that face in the mirror and say, "I love you" (if you can't say that, then say, "Jesus loves you," because that's certainly true).

• Do something different in the morning. Put on two different color socks, wear tennis shoes with your suit, sit at a different chair at the breakfast table, write a poem, go to work in a different way this morning. Somehow break the normal routine of your morning.

• Tell each member of your family one reason why you're glad they're in your family.

• Tell Jesus one reason why you're glad he's your Lord.

• Think of five reasons you're glad that you're you,

i.e., five things you like about yourself, and thank God for them.

• Look around your house. I mean *look* around your house, and, before you leave for the day, think of one thing that you're grateful for. Don't forget it when you get caught up in that day's problems.

• Pray for someone. You'll be amazed at what it does for his or her life as well as for yours.

• Choose one word or one line of Scripture and follow it for the day. In other words, if you choose the word *peace,* or *joy,* or *Lord,* then really try and contemplate that all during the day. Write it down on scraps of paper so it'll remind you of something. Put it on your dashboard. Put it on your desk, but as much as you can during the day, try to make it a living reality in your life. Or choose a phrase such as *Patient endurance* and give the world living proof that Jesus is real in that way in your life. Or choose a sentence such as *No condemnation now hangs over the head of those who are "in" Christ Jesus* (Rom. 8:1). And remember that you are free. Put flesh and bone on it. Dance to its music. Celebrate its reality. You will be amazed at how different Scripture will become in your life if you do this on a regular basis.

• Make it a point to meet someone new before lunchtime. You never know what might happen.

• Phone your mate in the morning, whether at the office or at home, and just tell him or her how much you love them. Have no other reason for phoning, except to say how glad you are that God chose them for you to live out your life with.

• Thank someone who works at your office, or who services your home, for contributing to your life. For example, thank that secretary who answers all the phone calls. If you get a chance, thank the garbage man for picking up your garbage. Stick a note on the mailbox for the mailman, just saying thanks for all the good news he brings each day. There are countless people in our lives to whom we forget to say thank you. This morning pick just one and tell him how much you appreciate him.

And what about the afternoon? Do you still subscribe to the notion that afternoons are "supposed" to be dull? I don't know who invented that myth, but he must be a millionaire by now because he has a lot of followers. (I think it was his brother who invented the one about Mondays.)

The afternoon often starts with lunch. Why not do something different today? Go to a different place to eat, or go to the same place, but with someone else.

● Tell the waitress that she's really doing a fine job, or leave her a note with your tip. Or really, I mean really, enjoy your food—focus in on it, taste it, explore it, instead of exploiting it. Take time to thank God for it. And if possible, try not to hurry through it.

● Go on a picnic during lunch. You might say, "That's impossible because I work downtown." Then sit on a park bench or a bench by the bus stop, and eat a sack lunch, and watch the people go by. It might give you a whole new perspective on life.

● Take a few minutes out of your lunch break to read a couple pages of something special—something that will inspire you to move into the afternoon with a little more power. It's a shame how frequently we exploit God's resources by being prejudiced against the afternoon (that is, in assuming we really can't get that much done in the afternoon). A friend told me that when he worked in Washington, D.C., he always had to get to people in the morning if he wanted to get something done because they were usually so ineffective in the afternoon. Be different. Be His.

• On your way back from lunch, find or buy a flower to give to your secretary, your wife, or to your child. Life is made up of little commitments, not big ones. And life is made up of little lumps of happiness. It's a real mistake when we wait and wait and wait for the big things to change our life—when in actuality, it's all the consistent little things that make life magic.

• Take thirty seconds out of your afternoon to be thankful for one thing at the office or at home.

• Ask somebody a good question today. What is their most important priority? What is their reason for being alive? Or, is what they're doing now moving towards their ultimate goal in life? Or, what are the three things that make them happiest? Or, any kind of question that helps you figure out what makes them tick and helps *them* figure out what makes them tick.

• Write your philosophy of life on a button and wear it for a day. You might get some interesting responses.

• Pick one word that means something special to you, that's important to you, and try to define it. Set it on your desk. (For example, *love, peace, hope, trust, freedom, gratitude*—what do they really mean to you?) Peace, for example, was once defined by a friend of mine as "the absence of envy." What would it mean to live a life without comparison?

• Take three minutes out of your busy schedule and try and write somebody a note today.

• Think of twelve reasons why you're glad to be alive.

Evening is really a special time of day. It's a time to relax, refocus. Time to be with your family. A time to think about what life is really all about. Hopefully, it's a time to be happy. Here are a couple of ideas to help cheer up your evening.

• Did you take any time to get some exercise today?

135

ENOUGH IS MORE THAN ENOUGH

One of the most important ways to stay alive and enjoy life is to get that oxygen and blood to pump through your body. If you haven't, go out for a short walk. Take someone from your family. Go for a little run if you can, or ride a bike. Jump rope or do something to make your heart beat.

• Help set the table in a different way tonight. Maybe you'll find some flowers in the yard and put them in the center. Maybe you'll make little name tags for everybody so they can sit down and make dinner look official and special. Maybe you'll put on some music that will help everybody relax. Maybe you'll get everybody to dress up a little bit and help celebrate how very special eating together is.

• Have everyone share one thing they're thankful for at dinner. Again, gratitude is the basic attitude of happiness.

• Have someone different say grace tonight.

• If you want to try something really unusual, try eating with your opposite hand tonight. (It's also a good way to learn how to eat more slowly, which is a good way to cut down on some of your calorie intake.)

• Instead of your usual grace for meals, thank God for each thing on the table. When was the last time you thanked him for forks, knives, spoons, napkins, for salt or coffee? Learning to thank him for the little things creates a joyful heart.

• Have a gripe-and-appreciation session during dinner. That means, it's legal to share either a special thing you appreciate about each other or something you have difficulty with. It does magical things to open up conversation.

• If you really want to be weird, sing a Christmas carol. Even though it's July, you'll remember that Christmas comes every day of the year if you choose to make it so.

● After dinner, do something unusual, like help mom pick up the dishes and maybe even get them washed. Maybe you can even make it a celebration.

● When was the last time your family played a game together after dinner? There are hundreds of simple games; for instance, take a piece of paper and have one person start by drawing the head of an animal and then pass it to the next person. They draw another part of the animal, and then pass it around and around and around until you see what you come up with. It's usually good for a laugh.

Or see how many things you can make with match sticks. Maybe you'll even bring home a game of puzzles and things that you can play. But every once in a while try and *participate* with your family in something, rather than just watching TV. Maybe you'll go outside and have a water balloon fight or play catch or go for a walk around the block or bring something to the neighbors. Doing things together doesn't seem like much at the time, but in the long run, it pays off.

● If your children are younger, have a parade through your house. Sounds silly, docsn't it? It is!

● When was the last time you put on a record, laid on the floor, and just absorbed the music? When you did nothing else but just listened, and enjoyed the privilege of having ears that can hear, and let every fiber of your being relax and rejoice?

● Make a little love note for someone in your family and hide it somewhere where they will be sure to find it in the morning. If the surprise doesn't cause them to have a heart attack, it may change their whole day.

● Write down a little passage of Scripture and maybe tape it to the mirror so someone sees it in the morning. Or put it next to their breakfast cereal bowl. Or tuck it inside your husband's business calendar. Or tape it up above the sink where your wife will be washing dishes that day. But in someway, try and help them remember that you love them and that God loves them, too.

MINUTE VACATIONS

Most of us overlook the minutes of our days without realizing that these moments are the very substance of our lives.

What do you do with these tiny capsules of time, these sixty-second pieces? They are usually found while waiting for a train, a bus, a doctor, or a cashier. Many ignore them or endure them as necessary boredom instead of utilizing them as opportunities to be stimulated, creative, relaxed. They can be a time when we expand our consciousness, develop our senses, and focus our attention like a beam of a flashlight on those things that are really important to us. They can become precious times of remembering, or intense times of funneled living, rather than just a time of waiting.

Take, for example, the inevitability of television commercials. Someone has calculated that by the time a young person is in high school, he or she will have viewed over eighteen thousand of them. At one to two minutes each, that's a lot of time. Have you ever considered doing more than just enduring them? For example, Tim Gaffney does exercises during commercials. In a thirty-minute to one-hour program, he can do 100 sit-ups and push-ups. Along the same line, you could stretch during the commercials—or for that matter, you could even do stretching exercises sometimes during the program. Some people read books of short little aphorisms, read the paper, knit, write letters, wrestle with the kids, or do minor fix-it repairs during commercials. Eliminate the concept of "lost time."

Odd pieces of time occur everywhere, like little jewels scattered throughout your day. What about those minutes before dinner? Ever thought of taking a photo from the evening paper and asking your six year old to try to guess "what's going on here?" If things like this are done consistently around your home, your children get into the habit of being imaginative. Have them make up a little story that fits the picture.

And what about the whole lost art of asking *good* questions? What about having your children try to describe their day with a color, and explain why? What about the simple but thought-provoking way of eliciting dialogue by finding out what the high point of the day was? Talking about the low points might turn into a discussion on creative problem solving.

A friend of mine used to do a very unique thing at dinner. Before anyone could eat, each person had to share one new thing he had learned that day. And if he didn't have anything new, he had to go get the dictionary and look up a word so he could share something about the newness of life during that day. Pretty soon it became a regular occasion, and you'd be amazed at how much it helped all their family grow.

Minute vacations soon become far more significant than we think. "Habits" of good questions, learning something new every day, expanding vocabulary, and imagination can have not only strong educational value but strong relational value as well. A sunrise may seem insignificant, until you don't have them anymore.

What about short readings from a book of poems, or a special verse from the Book itself? Minute vacations are the time of quiet miracles.

ENOUGH IS MORE THAN ENOUGH

What about creating the kind of atmosphere in which you might ask your six-year-old daughter to try to figure out where peas come from? Or having your college-age son explain how a felt tip pen is made and processed? How about dad taking a minute vacation to explain how a gas stove works, or mom sharing why a balanced meal is important to health? None of these require special training or special times. They don't take much planning, or even a lot of extra energy. In fact, they might become a source of new energy for your family.

Minute vacations are tremendous opportunities to explore our senses, which might just atrophy otherwise. A minute vacation might be spent, for example, picking up a nearby object such as a book or flower. How would you describe its shape, its texture, its nuances of colors?

Focusing on any one sense can be a minute learning adventure, a chance to develop and refine the very channels of input we so often ignore. What are you smelling right now? Feeling? Listen with your whole body for a moment—what do you hear? All other things being equal, we tend to see and hear only what we want to, or expect to—which can result in nearly mute days. A good, and fun, test of these abilities is to do such things as draw the face of your watch from memory, or draw an exact replica of your car. Though you have looked at both a thousand times, you will be amazed how much detail will be left out. What did your wife wear yesterday? How many prongs are there on a fork? Is the gas cap of your car on the right side or the left? What's an orange taste like? Could you tell a friend from another culture about an avocado—without using your hands?

Are there minutes in your day that you could convert into vacations? Are you still, maybe even unknowingly, practicing being unhappy?

Sometimes life is not so much to be understood as it is

to be lived out. Some of us spend more time analyzing life than we do living it. I need to remind you that joy is something you *are*. It's another way in which we express our gratitude for the one who lives within us and allow him to be expressed into a world that needs so many things. But it especially needs our grateful joy. I also need to remind all of us that it takes practice, practice, practice. Just like anything else, it will soon become a habit, and we can and will become contagiously happy.

The purpose of all this is to encourage you to both say and experience the words *Hallelujah . . . anyway*. Even if it's Monday. Even if it's six-thirty in the morning. Even if your washer ate the socks again, for the third time this week. Even if your car died the week after your warranty expired. Even if your vacations are only fifteen minutes long these days.

Why spend so much energy "putting our lives back together"? Maybe this little story will be a good reminder. A father came home late one evening, exhausted. Heading for the easy chair, he picked up the evening paper, looking forward to a few moments' rest. No sooner had he hit the chair than his young son joined the newspaper on his lap. "Can we play, dad?"

The father loved his son very much but really felt he needed some time alone. Noticing a picture in the paper that evening from a recent moonprobe, he came up with a plan. It was a photo of the earth, taken from the moon. He cut the picture out and then cut it into small pieces, creating an instant jigsaw puzzle. Almost all the pieces looked alike. He encouraged his son to take it to his room with some tape and put the earth back together again.

The father was satisfied that he would have more than enough time to relax. He was quite surprised to see his son appear about ten minutes later—with the photograph of the earth intact.

ENOUGH IS MORE THAN ENOUGH

"How did you do that so quickly?" he asked. "It was easy, dad," the boy replied. "There was a picture of a man on the back—and when I put the man together, the world came together."

15
THE
SECOND FIRE

For all that has been–Thanks.
To all that shall be–Yes!

Dag Hammarskjold
Markings

WHEN I INVITED CHRIST into my life, I, in a sense, lit the fire. But obviously, there is more to the Christian life than one step of faith. The process continues. The colors of each season get both deeper and brighter. The second fire is the one you light as you commit yourself to a journey of excellence in Jesus Christ, when you choose to remain on the growing edge where life is more significant, and more dangerous.

It requires discipline. It also requires tenacity. The prefix *re*, meaning "again," begins to preface much of your vocabulary: rededicate, rediscover, rebound, receive, redefine, reflect, refresh, regenerate. You realize the necessity of this process, else your work becomes simply ornamental and your leisure just analgesic.

ENOUGH IS MORE THAN ENOUGH

Keep on relighting the fire.

It will probably be as difficult as you imagine. Maybe more. Resistance will come from the most surprising places. As you seek to explore not only your country but yourself, many will in subtle ways try to seduce you back into mediocrity—because it's much less threatening. It's also much less enjoyable.

Late in his life John Steinbeck, winner of the Nobel Prize, decided to travel around the country he loved to explore it more deeply, to enjoy it more deeply, and in the process perhaps to write some of his discoveries. Interestingly enough, very few people encouraged him to go. Friend after friend reminded him of his age and the difficulties involved. He received the usual lectures about slowing down, losing weight, limiting his cholesterol intake, and basically not pursuing any more adventure or even excellence because it was simply too late in his life. "And I had seen so many," he wrote, "begin to pack their lives in cotton, wool, smother their impulses, hood their passions and gradually retire from their manhood into a kind of spiritual and physical semi-invalidism. In this they were even encouraged by their wives and relatives, and it's such a sweet trap."

He knew the potential problems of driving ten or twelve thousand miles alone in a truck with only his dog. But as he said, he was not about to surrender fierceness for a small gain in yardage. And at this point in his life, he was not about to begin trading in quality for quantity. He went. His adventures were recorded in a book called *Travels with Charlie in Search of America.*

Much of it betrays the sad, cellophane age we live in, so safe and sterile, and the profound consequences of such a life (or should I say lifelessness?).

"It was all plastic too—the table linen, the butter dish, the sugar and crackers were wrapped in cellophane, the jelly in a small plastic coffin sealed with cellophane. It was early evening and I was the only customer. Even the waitress wore a sponge apron. She wasn't happy, but then she wasn't unhappy. She wasn't anything."

On different occasions throughout the book, Steinbeck observes how insulated our society has become, and how we allow mediocrity to infuse our style of living.

Before he left, one of his friends, a well-known and highly respected political reporter (and as Steinbeck describes him, "a completely honest man") told him, "If anywhere in your travels you come on a man with guts, mark the place. I want to go see him. I haven't seen anything but cowardice and expediency. This used to be a nation of giants. Where have they gone? You can't defend a nation with a board of directors. That takes men. Where are they?"[1]

There are no shortcuts for character, and one of the best things we could do with our leisure time would be to pursue the quality and excellence of life-style that our country and our community needs.

John Gardner, author of *Excellence,* said, "The society which scorns excellence in plumbing because plumbing is a humble activity and tolerates shoddiness in philosophy because it is an exalted activity will have neither good plumbing nor good philosophy. Neither its pipes nor its theories will hold water."[2]

Many would agree that there is a real tendency these days towards boredom and mediocrity; few are willing to make the investment necessary for excellence. Sometimes, possibly, we're simply too tolerant, and we must remember that God does have a distaste for mediocrity. Scripture compels us to do each thing as if it were for Christ himself. All too often we allow Good to become the enemy of Best in both our work and our leisure. And we conveniently ignore Scriptures about working heartily, living abundantly, and God spewing out lukewarm lives.

The commitment to excellence requires that we first of all discover our gifts, but then invest them with abandonment.

Two stories illustrate the attitude necessary for a life of fulness and excellence.

A young man longed to see God. He had heard for many years of a wise old man who lived in the mountains nearby. After searching elsewhere for God in vain, the young man finally went to talk with the old man.

"Old man, tell me, how can I see God?"

The old man stopped, and looked at him deeply. He immersed himself in thought. The young man waited for what seemed like an eternity. Finally:

"Young man, I don't think that I can be of help to you, for you see I have a problem that is quite different. I can't *not* see Him."

The second fire, the touch of disciplined grace, washes away the imagined barriers between secular things and spiritual things and reintroduces the whole universe to us as God's. We begin to see the world and its people and events as Christ sees them. We allow him to be our 20/20 vision—and with a combination of discipline and grace we move closer to the central Yes of our lives.

The second story deals with our capacity to hear.

An Indian was in downtown New York, walking along with his friend, who lived in New York City. Suddenly he said, "I hear a cricket."

"Oh, you're crazy," his friend replied.

"No, I hear a cricket. I do! I'm sure of it."

"It's the noon hour. You know there are people bustling around, cars honking, taxis squealing, noises from the city. I'm sure you can't hear it."

"I'm sure I do." He listened attentively and then walked to the corner, across the street, and looked all around. Finally on the other corner he found a shrub in a large cement planter. He dug beneath the leaf and found a cricket.

His friend was duly astounded. But the Indian said, "No. My ears are no different from yours. It simply depends on what you are listening to. Here, let me show you."

He reached into his pocket and pulled out a handful of change—a few quarters, some dimes, nickels, and pennies. And he dropped it on the concrete.

Every head within a block turned.

"You see what I mean?" the Indian said as he began picking up his coins. "It all depends on what you are listening for."

As you seek to live a life of excellence, a life of godly intensity and verve, may you have eyes to see and ears to hear. But most important, may you have the wisdom to know what to look for and listen to.

NOTES

CHAPTER 1
1. M. C. Richards, *Centering: In Pottery, Poetry, and the Person* (Middletown, CT: Wesleyan University Press, 1962), p. 6.

CHAPTER 2
1. Nikos Kazantakis, *Zorba the Greek* (New York: Ballantine Books, 1952), p. 61.
2. Walter Kerr, *The Decline of Pleasure* (New York: Simon and Schuster, 1962), p. 11.
3. Kazantakis, *Zorba*, p. 334.

CHAPTER 3
1. Gordon Dahl, *Work, Play, and Worship in a Leisure-Oriented Society* (Minneapolis: Augsburg Publishing House, 1972), p. 12. I am indebted to Dahl for several ideas in this chapter.
2. Thomas Carlyle, *Past and Present*, 1843, quoted in *The Great Quotations*, George Seldes, ed. (New York: Pocket Books), p. 985.
3. Seldes, *The Great Quotations*, p. 575.
4. Ibid, p. 985.
5. Henry David Thoreau, *The Illustrated World of Thoreau*, Howard Chapnick, ed. (New York: Grosset and Dunlap, 1974), p. 20.
6. William McNamara, "Wasting Time Creatively," cassette tape from Spiritual Life Institute, Star Route One, Sedona, AZ.

CHAPTER 4
1. Karl Olsson, *Come to the Party* (Waco, TX: Word Books, 1972), p. 16.

CHAPTER 5
1. Walter B. Knight, *Three Thousand Illustrations for Christian Service* (Grand Rapids: Willian B. Eerdmans Publishing Co., 1947), p. 120.

CHAPTER 6

1. Dwight Carlson, *Run, Run, Run and Not Be Weary* (Old Tappan, NJ: Fleming H. Revell, 1974), pp. 26f.

2. Mary Keelan, *Full Circle Playbook* (Collegeville, MN: Full Circle Association [Liturgical Press], 1970), p. 40.

CHAPTER 7

1. Leslie B. Flynn, *It's About Time* (Newtown, PA: Timothy Books, 1974), p. 39.

2. William McNamara, *The Human Adventure* (Garden City, NY: Doubleday and Co., 1974), p. 53.

3. Flynn, *It's About Time,* p. 24.

4. Michel Quoist, *Prayers of Life* (M. H. Gill and Son Ltd., Dublin: 1965), pp. 76-78.

CHAPTER 9

1. Kazantakis, *Zorba,* pp. 138-9.

2. Mark Link, *Take Off Your Shoes* (Niles, IL: Argus Communications. 1972), p. 107.

CHAPTER 10

1. Victor Frankl, *The Doctor and the Soul* (New York: Bantam Books. 1952), p. xiii.

2. Larry Dean Olson, *Outdoor Survival Skills* (Provo, UT: 1976). p. 4.

CHAPTER 11

1. Joan Anglund, *A Cup of Sun* (New York: Harcourt Brace, 1967), p. 15.

2. A. A. Milne, *The House at Pooh Corner* (New York: Dell Books, 1970).

CHAPTER 12

1. Rosie Dosti, "Vacation Diet: Plan a Strategy," *Los Angeles Times,* June 8, 1978, p. 29.

CHAPTER 13

1. Fynn, *Mister God, This Is Anna* (New York: Ballantine Books, 1974).

2. Link, *Take Off Your Shoes,* p. 110.

3. Ibid, p. 112.

CHAPTER 14

1. McNamara, *The Human Adventure,* p. 74.

2. Lloyd Ogilvie, *Drumbeat of Love* (Waco, TX: Word Books, 1976), p. 112.

3. Ibid, p. 108.

CHAPTER 15

1. John Steinbeck, *Travels With Charley* (New York: Bantam Books, 1961), pp. 20-21, 45, 168.

2. John Gardner, *Excellence* (New York: Harper and Row, 1971).

Especially for people
who say,
"I need to read *When I
Relax I Feel Guilty*, but
I don't have the
time...."

Hear Tim Hansel share
the heart of this book in
a great audio experience

Three hours of life-changing listening

45021/A5407
ISBN 1-55513-079-8

from **LifeJourney Books**
a division of David C. Cook Publishing Co.
Elgin, Illinois / Weston, Ontario

Let your friends discover the wonder and joy of really living

Benefit from Tim's insights by using the study guide with a group of friends in your home or your church. *When I Relax I Feel Guilty* study kit, complete with book, guide and three-hour tape from Tim.

45013/A5406
ISBN 1-55513-501-3

from **LifeJourney Books**
a division of David C. Cook Publishing Co.
Elgin, Illinois / Weston, Ontario

How To Manage Your Time
How To Stop Living For Applause — John Holland
Making Time Making Money — Rita Davenport
Personal Power — Anthony Robbins
ON The Run: a newsletter for Busy Families
Univ. of Md. Extension
Laugh your Way To Success — Rita Davenport

Maxine Hancock is an author and conference speaker. Her most recent book is "Reevaluating Your Commitments." She and her husband, Campbell, have four grown